CHRIST'S SOLITARY THRONE

Christ's Solitary Throne

J. OSWALD SANDERS

KINGSWAY PUBLICATIONS
EASTBOURNE

ISBN 0 86065 462 1

Unless otherwise indicated, biblical quotations are from
the New International Version, © New York International
Bible Society 1978.

Front cover photo: Art Directors Photolibrary — London

Printed in Great Britain for
KINGSWAY PUBLICATIONS LTD
Lottbridge Drove, Eastbourne, E. Sussex BN23 6NT by
Cox & Wyman Ltd, Reading.
Typeset by CST, Eastbourne, E. Sussex.

Contents

	Introduction	7
1.	Christ's Solitary Throne	9
2.	The Purpose of Christ's Incarnation	25
3.	The Purpose of Christ's Temptation	39
4.	The Purpose of Christ's Cleansing of the Temple	53
5.	The Purpose of Christ's Transfiguration	67
6.	The Purpose of Christ's Death	79
7.	The Purpose of Christ's Resurrection	91
8.	The Purpose of Christ's Post-Resurrection Ministry	105
9.	The Purpose of Christ's Ascension	117
10.	The Purpose of Christ's Exaltation	129
11.	The Purpose of Pentecost	141
12.	The Purpose of Christ's Church	155
13.	The Purpose of Christ's Second Advent	167
	Index of Persons	179
	Scripture Index	181
	Notes	185

Introduction

In my earlier book, *The Incomparable Christ*, I aimed to give a doctrinal treatment of the great facts relating to the Person and work of Christ, but with a devotional slant, and in a form suited to the average Christian reader not deeply versed in theology.

This book has a different emphasis. The first chapter highlights the uniqueness and solitary grandeur of the Lord of glory. The chapters that follow concern twelve aspects of His life and ministry which contribute to His immense moral and spiritual stature and incredible achievements; but they are viewed more from the subjective than the objective angle. Special emphasis is placed on the underlying purpose behind the critical experiences of His life, and their practical relevance to a Christian living in the space age. Their significance to the Lord Himself is not overlooked.

It is my hope that these pages will help to bring the reader within the inner circle of the Lord's intimates.

J. OSWALD SANDERS

I
CHRIST'S SOLITARY THRONE

The Son of Man sits on his glorious throne (Mt 19:28).

Who is this Jesus Christ who said that if He were lifted up He would draw all men to Him? In what respect is Jesus Christ on a solitary throne? In what respect is Jesus Christ the Alpha and the Omega, the first and the last, the beginning and the end of all human thought, and of all human ideals in religion? . . . In what sense is Christ different from all other religious leaders and personalities? What is His pre-eminence?[1]

It was Dr Samuel Marinus Zwemer, one of the greatest missionaries to the Muslims, who posed these questions; questions which he had to face in matching the claims of Jesus with those of the False Prophet. And they are questions to which we too must have an answer if our faith is to be intelligent.

Many who greatly admire the human Jesus, are unwilling to concede to Him *a solitary throne.* Among them was the great Indian patriot and mystic, Mahatma Mohandas Ghandi. 'I cannot place Christ on a solitary throne,' he said, 'because I believe God has been incarnate again and again.'[2] He would willingly have accorded Him a throne on a level with that of Buddha, or Confucius, or Muhammad or Zoroaster; but a solitary throne? No!

And yet Christ demands nothing less than this, for 'He is Lord of all', and 'to Him every knee shall bow'. If we claim pre-eminence for Christ, it is no more than He claimed for Himself. Can we not detect in His teaching an egotism, a self-assertion that in anyone else would be considered laughable, if not objectionable? Then why does it sit so naturally and appropriately on Him?

One of the astounding features of His Sermon on the Mount, is the confident manner in which He claimed superiority and precedence over all the prophets and religious leaders who had gone before Him. With utter assurance He challenged and dismissed their interpretations of Scripture and substituted His own. He even had the temerity to make sweeping promises on behalf of God, for example: 'Ask and it will be given to you; seek and you will find; knock and the door will be opened to you' (Lk 11:9).

When the Pharisees challenged Him for what they considered His lax attitude towards the Sabbath, He replied by claiming that He was Lord, even of the Sabbath (Mk 2:28). He affirmed that He was greater than Solomon, Israel's most glorious monarch. He even asserted His pre-existence in the cryptic words, 'Before Abraham was, I existed.'

He employed a wealth of metaphors and imagery in relation to Himself that would mark Him out as unique. 'I am the good shepherd', 'I am the light of the world', 'I am the bread of life'. So audacious and absolute were His claims that we are left with only two options—either He was a deluded megalomaniac, or He was what He claimed to be—the Son of God.

If the Gospel records, which attribute to Him a divine origin, are true, then we have a plausible explanation for His amazing life and ministry. But if this is denied, how can we account for the unique life and teaching that have deeply influenced and indeed shaped the art, music, literature and architecture of the whole world? What explanation is there for His miracle-working power?

Many valid reasons in support of our Lord's claims to uniqueness and pre-eminence can be adduced.

His birth was without parallel

Three hundred and fifty thousand babies are born every day. What was there about this baby, born of humble parents in an obscure eastern village, to cause a world of men two millennia removed to stop and take note of His birthday? Why reckon history and date correspondence from that day? Why celebrate it with lavish gifts, sumptuous feasts and illuminated cities? Why is the music of that week each year dominated the world around by carols about His birth? These facts are true of no other baby and demand explanation. Why are they true of Him?

> It was a happy thought of Dionysius, a theologian and astronomer of the sixth century, to introduce a Christian era, dating all events, not from the founding of Rome, but B.C. and A.D., making the manger at Bethlehem the centre of all history. Today that era has become almost universal.

1. Of no other baby could it be affirmed that its birth was not the beginning of its existence. Logically, if Jesus had no existence prior to His birth, then there was no incarnation of the Son of God—only the birth of one more human being, remarkable though He be. And if there was no true incarnation, then there is no Saviour, only another sinful man who needed salvation himself.

2. He was the only baby conceived without a human father. If, as some assert, He did have a human father, it follows that He was not the second Person of the Trinity. He was only the natural son of immoral parents, born out of wedlock; for Joseph claimed Jesus was not his son. To put it another way, Jesus was the only baby to be born of a virgin.

But is this so surprising if Christ is indeed God as He claimed? Was it likely that this event for which God had been making meticulous preparations for four thousand years would occur in the ordinary course of nature? It has been well argued that if, as science demands, every effect must have an adequate cause, then the presence of a sinless Man in the midst of a world of universally sinful men surely implies a miracle of origin. Such a Man as Jesus was, demands some such birth as the Gospels record.

Luke's Gospel attributes our Lord's conception to the supernatural agency of the Holy Spirit. The angel announced to Mary, 'The Holy Spirit will come upon you, and the power of the Most High will overshadow you. So the holy one to be born will be called the Son of God' (1:35).

3. *He was the only baby of whom it could be claimed that He was more than man.* Jesus referred to Himself both as Son of Man and Son of God. One Person, yet possessing two natures—the God-man. However, He was no schizophrenic, for His two natures were so totally united as to constitute Him a single Person who acted with a single consciousness and will.

4. *Of no other baby could it be said that His death was the supreme purpose of His birth.* To all others, death is unwelcome but inevitable, something to be postponed for as long as possible. To Jesus, death was avoidable, but deliberately chosen: 'No-one takes it [my life] from me, but I lay it down of my own accord. I have authority to lay it down and authority to take it up again' (Jn 10:18).

His claims were fantastic

What normal man would make the astounding claims that Jesus did, and expect to be believed?

1. He claimed to be the only way of approach to God, the sole channel of truth and life. 'I am the way and the truth and the life. No-one comes to the Father except through me' (Jn 14:6).

No claim could be more definite, more absolute, more startling. In one sweeping assertion He brushed aside all other religious leaders. No other founder of a world religion has been so rash. Spoken by someone without the moral authority our Lord possessed, and unsupported by the quality of life He displayed, His claim would have seemed as puerile as that of Idi Amin of Uganda when he claimed to be the most powerful man in the world.

2. He asserted that He was the full and final revelation of God, expressed in terms of human life. In His words and acts and attitudes, men could see the words and acts and attitudes of God. 'I and my Father are one.' 'Anyone who has seen me has seen the Father.' 'The words I say to you *are not just my own.* Rather, it is the Father, living in me, who is doing his work' (Jn 14:10, italics mine).

3. He claimed to have the power to forgive sin. The full significance of this claim was not lost on the Pharisees. 'Who can forgive sin but God only?' they blustered. Exactly! Since only the person sinned against can forgive a sin, Christ's claim meant that He was asserting His full deity. He implied that all sin was committed against Him, and He alone had power to forgive it. For this blasphemy, they were more than ever determined to do away with Him.

In spite of the fantastic nature of Christ's claims, they have been believed and acted on by countless millions down the ages.

He appropriated singular titles

In the vision granted to John and recorded in the first chapter of the Book of the Revelation, the glorified Christ assumes to Himself five distinctive titles, and makes assertions that further support His claim to be unique.

1. *'I am the Alpha and the Omega'* (v.8), a metaphor implying completeness. He claims to be the Director of the whole course of world history. As has often been pointed out, between alpha and omega, the first and the last letters of the Greek alphabet, lies every possibility of human thought and speech. Christ claims this absoluteness for Himself.

2. *'I am the First and the Last'* (v.17), the origin and goal of all creation. All things will end with Christ, even as they began with Him. Since there was no God before Him, He is the first. As there will be no other after Him, He is the last. In relation to His people, He is both the author and finisher of their faith.

3. *'I am the living One; I was dead, and behold I am alive for ever and ever'* (v.18). This paradoxical statement enshrines two amazing thoughts. The One who died was alive before His birth in Bethlehem. The Living One became dead, yet is now alive. Because He defeated death, He is able to deliver men from the bondage of their fear. Christ here contrasts the eternal life that is inherent in Him, and His voluntary surrender to the powers of death.

4. *'I am alive for evermore'* (v.18). Death was powerless to hold its prey. Lazarus was raised from the dead, only to be grasped in its cold clutch once again. Christ was raised from the dead, but now lives in the power of an endless life. It is this glorious fact that provides the basis of our hope of eternal life. The Church could not live if Christ were dead, but because Christ lives, the Church cannot die.

5. *'I hold the keys of death and Hades'* (v.18), wrested from the hand of the tyrant who had the power of death, the devil. To the Jew, Hades was a prison-house to which death is the door. But our triumphant Lord now stands at the door of Hades, keys in hand, to conduct the redeemed into the glories of the life beyond.

His claims produce remarkable effects

Bishop Chandhu Ray (formerly of Pakistan, but later of Singapore), in telling of his search for Christ, said that Christianity was a foreign religion about which no one had ever spoken to him. For nine years he had been seeking the reality of God. Then a Christian friend of his had trouble with his eyes. His doctor told him he would operate in the hope of restoring at least some of his sight. The Bishop recounted:

> As can be imagined, my friend was very much perturbed at the possibility of losing his sight. When I visited him he said, 'I may never be able to read my Bible again. Will you read it to me?'
>
> I took his Bible, and it opened at the fourteenth chapter of John's Gospel. As I read aloud, I was amazed at the claims of Jesus—'I am the way, the truth and the life . . . He that has seen me has seen the Father . . . I am in the Father and the Father in me.' And then I read the promise of verse 14: 'If you ask anything in my name, I will do it.'
>
> I turned to my Christian friend and said, 'This Jesus of yours makes such amazing claims. Why don't you ask Him about your eyes?'
>
> My friend and I both knelt beside his bed and spent most of the night in prayer. That night I became conscious of the reality of God. I turned to my friend and told him that when he returned from the hospital seeing, I would follow Jesus. He grasped my hand and asked, 'Do you believe I will ever see again?' I replied that I believed God had given me my sight and his too.
>
> We went to the hospital next morning, a well-known hospital in Simla. A Scotsman was to do the surgery. When he first of all applied some instrument to measure the tension of the eyes, he found the tension reduced. Thinking something was wrong with the instrument, he sent for another, only to find that the tension was indeed reduced.
>
> 'What did this man put in his eyes last night?' the doctor asked me. 'When I examined his eyes last night, the tension was so high I decided to do the surgery this morning. Now the tension is greatly reduced.'

Then I knew that Jesus was really alive. I told the doctor about our prayers, and how we felt we were in the presence of God. The doctor shook his head and said, 'We don't believe in miracles.' After thinking a while, he added, 'Were many tears shed when you were praying?' 'We were very conscious of the presence of God,' I replied.

The doctor decided that it was the tears that had reduced the tension. He would not do the operation now, he said, but should the tension return, the operation would be necessary. The tension has never returned, and my friend's eyes cleared up gradually. We both knew that Jesus is alive.

It was Christ's stupendous claims for Himself that first kindled in Chandhu Ray's heart the spark of faith that led to his conversion and a singularly fruitful spiritual ministry.

His character was simple yet complex

Naturalistic philosophers and non-Christian historians have alike conceded the uniqueness of our Lord's character. Whether it is the voice of an Ernest Renan or of an H. G. Wells, the verdict is much the same. While unwilling to concede His deity, they rank Him foremost among men in symmetry of character and perfection of person. Here are some reasons for this.

1. Of all men, Christ alone has shown a character that is absolutely symmetrical, in which there is neither excess nor deficiency. And yet this very fact presents a difficulty to some thoughtful people.

Some have felt that the very perfection of Christ's character creates the chief difficulty in dealing with it. A character in which there are some outstanding excellences, even though it be accompanied by obvious faults, immediately strikes the attention and captures the fancy. But a character that is perfectly symmetrical and evenly balanced, is not readily appreciated as striking by the casual observer. Yet it is this very quality that belongs uniquely to the Christ portrayed in the Gospels.

2. *He was unique among men, in that He was sinless.*
Scripture everywhere either states or assumes His sinlessness. 'In Him is no sin'—essentially, asserts John. 'He
knew no sin'—experientially, claimed Paul. 'He did no
sin'—actually, affirmed Peter. 'He was tempted . . . yet
without sin,' wrote the author of the letter to the Hebrews.
'Can any of you prove me guilty of sin?' He Himself
asked—a challenge that was never taken up, even by His
disciples who lived with Him day and night.

3. *Unlike the holiest of men, He never shed a tear over
conscious failure or evinced the slightest discontent with
Himself or His achievements.* Yet He was the humblest of
men. Confucius mourned that in letters he was perhaps the
equal of other men; but he had not attained to the character
of the perfect man. No such confession passed the lips of
Jesus.

It is said that no man is a hero to his valet, yet the
disciples who kept company with Jesus on terms of closest
intimacy suffered no such disillusionment. They record no
discrepancy between His teaching and His private life.
Peter later referred to Him as 'the Holy One and just'.
Shaken with remorse, Judas cried, 'I have betrayed in-
nocent blood.' Awed at Christ's demeanour when suffering
in the crucible of the cross, the penitent thief gasped, 'This
man has done nothing wrong.'

4. *In Christ's attractive personality there was a singular
blending of contrasting virtues.* Though manifesting the
gentler graces of womanhood, He could not be charged
with effeminacy. His virile manhood caused Him to be
likened to the rugged Elijah and the austere John the
Baptist. He was the manliest of men.

His balance of character was seen as clearly in His
silences as in His speech, for, unlike ourselves, He never
spoke when it would be wiser to keep silent. His dignified
silence before the inquisitive Herod and the craven Pilate,

highlighted the inner strengths of His character.

In most great men there is one outstanding quality that lifts them above their fellows. In Job, it was his patience; in Moses, his meekness; in John, his love. But in Jesus there is no predominant grace or virtue—He is altogether lovely.

5. *Certain qualities of character that are not usually combined in the one person coalesced in Him.* For example, the unusual combination of strong independence, and yet of dependence on His Father. 'I can of my own self do nothing.' Indifferent to the praise or approval of the crowd though He was, His craving for the love and understanding of His own inner circle of friends was most moving. While He longed for their sympathy, He never became dependent on it.

Seeming incompatibles such as joy and sorrow coexisted in Him. Majesty and humility were wedded in His words and actions, qualities that were clearly manifested in the Upper Room, when Jesus, *knowing 'that he had come from God* and was returning to God . . . took off his outer clothing, and wrapped a towel round his waist . . . and began to wash his disciples' feet' (Jn 13:3–5, italics mine).

6. Other characteristics which have found expression in the life and character of every great teacher and religious leader, were conspicuously absent from His life. *He never sought advice from others.* So vast is the scope of all there is to be known, that the wisest men of every age have been glad to seek the advice and draw on the knowledge of those who have excelled in fields other than their own. Even Solomon and Moses drew on the skill, expertise and wisdom of their advisers. But on the few occasions when advice was tendered to Jesus, He gently rejected it.

He never apologized, or withdrew any statement He had made. When it is remembered that our Lord's teaching was extemporaneous, this is an amazing thing. In anyone else, failure to apologize or admit error would be a tragic blemish. Maturity of character is seen in a willingness to withdraw words that have proved wrong or to apologize. But in the case of our Lord, no such occasion arose.

He was unconcerned about justifying actions that appeared ambiguous. Although He was in the vicinity of the prison in which John the Baptist was languishing, Jesus offered no explanation of His failure to visit him. Instead, He sent a message: 'Happy is the man who does not find me a stumbling-block' (Mt 11:6, New English Bible).

He expressed no regret to Martha and Mary for remaining two days where He was, after receiving their urgent appeal to come to their brother in his illness. We would have rushed to his side, or at least justified our delay, but Jesus was more concerned with developing their faith. He refused to allow soft sentiment to mar the process.

He never confessed a sin. It is the holiest of men, not the renegades who are the most abject in their confessions of sin. Read the prayers of Bishop Lancelot Andrewes, or the Journal of David Brainerd, or the Diary of Andrew Bonar as they confess their failure to live up to even their own ideals. Jesus, on the contrary, invited the most searching scrutiny of His life.

He never invited the prayers even of His intimate friends. How different from Paul who pleaded: 'Brethren pray for us.' It is noteworthy that in the Garden of Gethsemane, Jesus asked His friends to *watch* with Him, but to *pray* for themselves (Lk 22:40; Mt 26:38).

His death was unprecedented

Our Lord's death was no less unique than His birth and His life. If 'the indescribable humility of God' is seen in the incarnation, how shall we describe the humility He displayed in the shameful episode of the cross? Several features mark it out as without precedent in history.

1. His was the only death that climaxed millennia of prophecy. A continuing stream of prophets, and an unceasing ritual of animal sacrifice foretold and foreshadowed the death of the Messiah. Even in the events that accompanied the crucifixion, no fewer than thirty-three Old Testament prophecies found their fulfilment, as a reverent comparison of such passages as Psalm 22 and Isaiah 53 will establish.

2. *Of no other person could it be said that his death was not inevitable.* To Him, as we have seen, death was not a necessity but a deliberate choice. Far from being overcome by death, Jesus summoned death to be His servant, when by an act of His will He dismissed His spirit (Mt 27:50). He emerged from the ordeal as Victor, not as victim.

3. *His death was unique in that it was accompanied by multiple miracles.* First there was *the mysterious darkness*. 'It was now about the sixth hour, and darkness came over the whole land until the ninth hour; for the sun stopped shining' (Lk 23:44–45).

This was no eclipse, as some have suggested. Whoever heard of an eclipse that lasted for three hours? Indeed, there is extra-biblical support for the fact that the sun was at its furthest distance from the moon when the Son of God expired. It was the act of a considerate, loving God, shielding the sufferings of His Son from impious eyes.

> Well might the sun in darkness hide,
>   And shut His glories in,
> When God, the mighty Maker died,
>   For man, the creature's sin.
>   *Isaac Watts*

Synchronizing with the expiring shout of triumph of the Son of God, *'the curtain of the temple was torn in two'* (Lk 23:45). The magnitude of this miracle is not always realized. The heavy curtain separating the Holy Place from the Holiest of All, measured sixty feet wide by thirty feet high. The woven material of which it was made was as thick as a hand. It was so heavy that it required three hundred men to hang it. The Jews claimed that a team of horses on either side, pulling in opposite directions, could not tear it apart. And yet it was suddenly torn from top to bottom by the hand of God in the gaze of the awe-stricken priests. Here was tangible evidence that 'the way into the holiest' had been opened to all believers.

A mighty earthquake also coincided with His death.

> The earth shook and the rocks split. The tombs broke open and the bodies of many holy people who had died were raised to life. They came out of the tombs, and after Jesus' resurrection they went into the holy city and appeared to many people (Mt 27:51–53).

Thus linked with His death were the evidences of His authority over Nature and His mastery of death. He is the Lord of life.

With this array of evidence before us, can we accord to Jesus of Nazareth, Son of God and Son of Man, anything but a solitary throne?

> The highest place that heaven affords
>   Is His by sovereign right,
> The King of kings, the Lord of Lords,
>   And heaven's eternal light.
> *Thomas Kelly*

The familiar words of the Apostles' Creed, 'born of the Virgin Mary', refer to quite opposite but mutually complementary truths. 'Born of Mary' tells us that beside a manger in the stable of an inn at ancient Bethlehem of Judea, a human child was born. In Jesus Christ we have no alien, no Mork from another planet, but one of us—flesh of our flesh and bone of our bone. Like us all, Jesus was formed in the womb of a woman, was brought into the world through the wonder of human birth, was nourished at his mother's breast and lived out his childhood in the midst of brothers, sisters and cousins . . .

In all these matters Jesus did not differ materially from the rest of us. He and you and I are one in the genuineness and fulness of our humanity.

But 'born of a virgin' points in the opposite direction. It is the sign that he was *different* from all the rest of us. Natural processes of humankind could never have brought him into being. The Virgin Birth stands as a label over the Christmas child: 'Not made by man.'[1]

Kenneth S. Kantzer

2

The Purpose of Christ's Incarnation

> The Word became flesh and lived for a while among us (Jn 1:14).

Shortly after Dr J. B. Phillips and Dr E. V. Rieu had completed their translations of the four Gospels into contemporary speech, I heard them being interviewed by the BBC. Each was asked by the compère, among other things, to tell what effect their immersion in the atmosphere of the Gospels over the period had had upon them.

Dr Rieu, a noted classical scholar, said simply, 'It changed me!' To the same question Dr Phillips replied, 'It resulted in the emergence of a Figure so much greater than man that I could only gasp incredulously. *In the incarnation, the incredible humility of God struck me with overwhelming awe!'*

The reason the New Testament writers regarded the incarnation—literally 'enfleshment'—of our Lord with such great importance, is found in the divine purpose behind that epochal event. This eternal purpose must carry tremendous implications for the human race since it moved the Son of God to empty Himself of the outward manifestations of His glory and clothe Himself with our humanity.

In the incarnation, the Eternal Son of God did not in any degree diminish or demean His divine nature. That world-shaking and life-changing event which took place in Bethlehem constituted one of the greatest miracles as well as one of the greatest crises of history. Who could conceive of the Infinite becoming 'an infant a span long'? Who could imagine the Son who 'fills heaven and earth' contracting Himself to the body of a tiny baby? Small wonder the angels veil their faces in the presence of so inscrutable a mystery.

The birth of Jesus has inspired some noble poetry which has enriched the Church. Among the finest is John Milton's Nativity Ode:

> That glorious form, that light insufferable,
> And that far-beaming blaze of majesty,
> Wherewith He wont, at heaven's high council
> To sit the midst of Trinal unity,
> He laid aside; and here with us to be,
> Forsook the courts of universal day,
> And chose with us a darksome house
>   Of mortal clay.

Another quaint early poet, George Herbert, depicted the scene when the Eternal Son rose from His throne to visit earth, in these vivid words:

> Hast Thou not heard what my Lord Jesus did?
> Then let me tell you a strange storie.
> The God of power, when He did ride
> In His majestick robes of glorie,
> Resolved to light; and so one day
> He did descend, undressing all the way.
> The starres His tires of light and rings obtained,
> The cloud His bow, the fire His spear,
> The sky His azure mantle gained.
> And when they asked what He would wear,
> He smiled, and said as He did go,
> He had new clothes amaking down below.

As he was contemplating the mysteries of the Christian faith, in awe and wonder the Apostle Paul exclaimed:

> Beyond all question, the mystery of godliness is great:
> *He appeared in a body*,
>   was vindicated by the Spirit,
>   was seen by angels,
>   was preached among the nations,
>   was believed on in the world,
>   was taken up in glory (1 Tim 3:16, italics mine).

One can sense the apostle's amazement at 'the incredible humility of God', when the Creator of the universe slipped unobtrusively into the stream of our humanity. Christmas is not Santa Claus, reindeer, trees and feasting—it is nothing less than this: God appeared in our midst in a frail human body—one of us! 'A more wonderful fact was never expressed in words, was never even conceived.'

'As the biblical context makes clear,' writes Kenneth S. Kantzer,

> no new person came into existence at the conception of the Virgin Mary. Rather, an eternal person, the second person of the Triune God, chose to come down into our human race and be born one of us. An eternal person in his own right, he took something new to himself—humanity, flesh and blood, our human life and nature—because he loved us unto salvation at a cross. Instead of an ordinary human baby, begotten by a man and born of a woman to produce a new person, the Spirit of God introduced into the body of Mary a Divine Person, who through the Virgin Birth added to himself all that is essential to humanity. This is the incarnation of the eternal God—God become also man—the mystery and the miracle of Christmas.[2]

The fact of the incarnation

Paradoxical though it may appear, the union of a human and a divine nature in the single Person of

Jesus of Nazareth, is taught with clarity and finality in the New Testament.

A paradox has been defined as 'a statement that seems at first to be absurd; something that conflicts with preconceived notions of the reasonable or the possible, but which nevertheless bears the unmistakable ring of truth'. Many truths are taught by paradox in Scripture, and the incarnation is one of them.

Our Lord is presented to us as One who was so truly human that He grew weary, and yet so divine that He fed five thousand with five loaves and two fish; so human that He wept over the death of His friend Lazarus, yet so divine that He raised him from the dead; so human that He died, yet so divine that He rose from the dead, leaving behind Him an empty cocoon of spice-impregnated grave clothes and an empty tomb.

But the Christian claim that the Word became flesh and lived among us has not gone unchallenged. Some religions require no factual and historical basis, but Christianity is not among them.

It is only of comparatively recent years that doubt has been thrown upon the historical existence of Christ. Philosophy has joined hands with science to consign Jesus to the realm of myth. It is not our purpose to try to refute the claims of this conspiracy, but the following quotations from non-Christian sources will serve to demonstrate that Christ's historicity is not endangered.

In the Tractate *Sanhedrin* (43a) of the Babylonian Talmud, this passage occurs:

> On the eve of the Passover, Jesus of Nazareth was hung. During the forty days a herald went before him crying aloud: 'He ought to be stoned because he practised magic, has led Israel astray and caused them to rise in rebellion. Let him who has something to say in his defence come forward and declare it'. But no one came forward, and he was hung on the eve of the Passover.

To this Jewish testimony may be added that of the Roman Tacitus, who in his *Annals* xv 44 wrote:

> Christus, the founder of the name, had undergone the death penalty in the reign of Tiberius, by sentence of the procurator Pontius Pilate, and the pernicious superstition was checked for the moment, only to break out once more, not merely in Judea, the home of the disease, but in the capital itself.

Thus extra-biblical testimony confirms the biblical assertion that the Word became flesh and actually dwelt among us.

As stated earlier, our Lord's birth did not mark His origin, only His appearance on the stage of history. Every other baby had entered the world as a new individual, but the new thing in His case was not His personality, but only His human body. As *the Logos* (Jn 1:1) He had existed from all eternity. In John's statement there is the presupposition of existence prior to the manifestation: 'The reason the Son of God appeared was to destroy the devil's works' (1 Jn 3:8). In any case, how could there be an incarnation if there were no previous existence? How could there be an Eternal Trinity if there were no pre-existent Son?

The timing of the incarnation

Chronologically, the first reference to the incarnation in the New Testament is found in Galatians 4:4:

> But when the time had fully come, God sent his Son, born of a woman, born under law, to redeem those under law, that we might receive the full right of sons.

This compact statement is pregnant with truths of theological importance. It tells us not only of the timing, but also the manner and purpose of the incarnation.

The importance God attached to this event may be gauged by the fact that it called for no less than four millennia of preparation. The expression 'the time had fully come' implies that the period God had purposed should elapse before sending His Son as Messiah was fulfilled, and now at this point He broke into history. It was the culmination of centuries of preparation and education of the Chosen People. The incarnation was no afterthought of God, designed to meet an emergency situation, but the maturing of an eternal purpose.

At last the divine discipline over the centuries had brought the rebellious and intransigent Hebrew nation to the consciousness that no matter how carefully they tried to observe the Mosaic code, they were totally unable to save themselves. They must look elsewhere for help.

As all students of church history know, the appropriate timing of the incarnation was remarkable. The stage was uniquely set for the rapid transmission of the Good News. It was no accident of history that the Roman Empire had in large measure maintained world peace and had constructed a wide-spreading network of roads that greatly facilitated travel for the heralds of the Gospel. Nor was it by chance that the rich and flexible Greek language was in use throughout the whole Empire. These and other factors made the moment chosen by God the most auspicious of all time for the manifestation on earth of His Son.

The manner of the incarnation

The clause 'born of a woman' implies that Jesus had a *human* mother, and thus inherited a fully human nature. 'Born under law' implies that he had a *Jewish* mother, and as a member of the Jewish nation He was therefore subject to Jewish law.

It is a noteworthy fact that although Paul does not make any specific reference to the fact that Christ was born of a virgin, whenever he referred to Christ's birth, he invariably used some unusual and significant expression that is entirely consistent with that fact. In Galatians 4, Paul employs the word 'born' three times (vv. 4, 23, 29), but he uses a different word when speaking of the birth of Jesus.

The mere fact that Jesus was born of a woman does not necessarily imply that He was virgin-born. For the revelation of that truth we look elsewhere.

Mary was greatly troubled when the angel told her that she would bear a son.

> 'How will this be,' Mary asked the angel, 'since I am a virgin?' The angel answered, 'The Holy Spirit will come upon you, and the power of the Most High will overshadow you. So the holy one to be born will be called the Son of God' (Lk 1:34–35).

While Paul's statement in Galatians 4:4 does not explicitly assert or prove the virgin birth of Christ, it is in full harmony with all the other Scriptures relating to that subject.

It is conceded that the Bible does not demand belief in the virgin birth as a prerequisite to salvation. But if it is only a myth or a legend and not an historical fact, then we are left with a purely human saviour born of sinful parents, and therefore not a member of the Holy Trinity. It is not the *knowledge* of the fact but rather its *reality and integrity* that provide the basis for our salvation. It is possible for a person to be saved without understanding the details of the process, just as a baby may be born of a mother who knows nothing of embryology. The *fact* of the virgin birth is an integral part of the Christian faith.

At the close of one of his services, a very popular preacher said, 'I want to assure you that I do not believe in the virgin birth of Christ, and I hope none of you do.' His sincerity is not in doubt, but is such a position logically, not to say biblically, tenable? A consideration of the alternatives open would seem to render such a view logically impossible. What are some of the alternatives?

If there were no virgin birth, the *New Testament records*

would be proved untrustworthy, and other doctrines would be thrown in doubt.

Instead of being 'blessed among women', *Mary would be branded as unchaste*, and Jesus the illegitimate child of immoral parents. Was God open to such an alternative as this?

Christ's pre-existence would be ruled out, with the inevitable corollary that there was no real incarnation; nor would He be the Second Person of the Trinity as the Scriptures assert.

It was essential to His work as Mediator on our behalf that the mode of His incarnation *should in no way impair or diminish His deity*. This end was secured by arresting the normal transmission of the racial heritage of a sinful nature through the miracle of the virgin birth. As the message of the angel to Mary predicted, it was through the activity of the Holy Spirit that this was achieved: 'The Holy Spirit will come upon you . . . so the holy one to be born will be called the Son of God (Lk 1:35).

The purpose of the incarnation

A review of the Scriptures relating to the incarnation reveals that it is almost always linked with redemption. As Martin Niemoller so picturesquely put it, the cradle and the cross of Christ were hewn out of the same tree.

In his first letter, the Apostle John discloses a fourfold purpose in the incarnation:

1. 'This is how God showed his love among us: He sent his one and only Son into the world *that we might live through him* (4:9). God sent His Son into the world so that through our union with Him in His death and resurrection, we who were dead in trespasses and sins 'may participate in the divine nature' (2 Pet 1:4).

2. 'He loved us and sent his Son *as an atoning sacrifice for our sins*' (4:10, italics mine). That is, to make amends for

our sins by undergoing the punishment they merited.

> The doctrine of propitiation is precisely this [wrote John Murray] that God loved the objects of His wrath so much that He gave His Son, to the end that He by His blood should make provision for the removal of this wrath. It was Christ's so to deal with the wrath, that the loved would no longer be the objects of wrath, and love would achieve its aim of making the children of wrath the children of God's good pleasure.

3. 'The Father has sent his Son *to be the Saviour of the world*' (4:14, italics mine). If Jesus were to 'taste death for every man', and thus 'save His people from their sins', He must of necessity enter the stream of their humanity. Because He did this, it can justly be claimed that in Christ, the Eternal God knew human life from the inside and by personal experience.

In walking through the streets of a city such as Calcutta with its teeming population, and where beggars abound, one cannot but be moved by their pitiable plight. It could well stir one to work to obtain relief for them, to compile heart-breaking statistics and make moving speeches on their behalf. But it would be an entirely different matter to *actually become a beggar* and share their lot. Yet this is exactly what our Lord did in the incarnation. Even God could fully know human life only by becoming human.

So fully did Jesus identify Himself with men in every aspect of their lives, that it could be claimed that 'there is not a note in the organ of our humanity that, when touched, does not find a sympathetic vibration in the mighty range and scope of our Lord's being'.

4. 'The reason the Son of God appeared was to destroy the devil's work' (3:8). The meaning of the word 'destroy' in this verse is the same as in Revelation 1:5, 'To Him who loves us and has freed us from our sins by His blood.' It means 'to dissolve or loosen'.

'Do not forget the meaning of the Advent historically,'

counselled G. Campbell Morgan.

> It was the invasion of human history by One who snatched the
> sceptre from the Usurper. It was the intrusion of forces into
> human history which dissolved the consistency of the works of
> the devil, and causes them to break and fail.[3]

5. *To prepare for a second appearing*. This might be
added to John's four reasons. In the letter to the Hebrews,
Christ's first and second advents are linked, and their purpose interpreted:

> So Christ was sacrificed once to take away the sins of many
> people; and *he will appear a second time*, not to bear sin, but to
> bring salvation to those who are waiting for Him (9:28, italics
> mine).

His first advent was for the purpose of dealing with and
destroying sin, but His second advent is not to deal with sin,
but to save those who are eagerly waiting for Him. When
He comes the second time, He will be crowned with glory,
not with thorns; with the sceptre of the universe in His
hand, not a reed of mockery; with radiant joy, no longer as
a Man of Sorrows. He will come to set up His kingdom that
will never pass away.

It can therefore be said that in His incarnation our Lord
perfectly unveiled and revealed His Father (Jn 14:9). He
brought to men a new consciousness of God, and purged
their minds of false conceptions of Him. He exemplified to
His contemporaries a type of humanity that was pure and
winsome. This was possible because sin is not an essential
constituent of human nature. He expiated our sins and thus
removed our haunting fear and guilt. He set us gloriously
free from sin, and turned the ever-receding mirage of an
attainable holiness into a vibrant reality. All these blessings
were the purpose and fruit of the incarnation.

> For the Maker, when the Foe
> Wrought His creature death and woe,

Bowed the heavens, came below;
And in the Virgin's womb His dwelling making,
Became true man, our very nature taking,
For He hath triumphed gloriously.

Anonymous

Jesus shows us that trust and obedience are the twin pillars of a successful operation against the devil. However the Tempter twisted and turned, and sought to dazzle him, Jesus never wavered in his trust in the Father, and never swerved in obedience to him. Satan bent all his wiles to achieve a millimetre of disobedience, of deviation from the true. He failed with Jesus, where he succeeded in Eden . . .

Jesus shows us that the use of Scripture in temptation is a powerful weapon. The devil is not afraid of us. He is afraid of all that speaks of God. The Scriptures do just that. If you want to overcome temptation regularly, habitually, I know no sharper weapon than the Word of God, studied, learned by heart and used in the moment of attack. Nor is this a matter of mere proof-texts. The way Jesus handles the devil's quotations of Scripture shows how the context was uppermost in his mind. He was not going to base his action on a verse from the Old Testament ripped from its context.[1]

Michael Green

3
The Purpose of Christ's Temptation

> At once the Spirit sent him out into the desert, and he was in
> the desert forty days, being tempted by Satan. He was with the
> wild animals, and angels attended him (Mk 1:12–13).

Temptation is a uniform experience of human life, and so it
is to be expected that it would form part of the experience
of the Son of Man if he were to be, in any real sense, a part
of the human race. Virtue, to be virtue, must be tested. The
unique thing is not so much that Christ was tempted, as that
He emerged from the ordeal unscathed and untainted by
sin. We are not true to the biblical record—and incidentally
to ourselves—if in our thinking we make a sharp distinction
between our Lord's temptation and our own.

The Lord's three temptations tie into His baptism. There
is significance in the juxtaposition of Matthew 3:16–17 and
4:1.

> At that moment heaven was opened, and he saw the Spirit of
> God descending like a dove and lighting on him. And a voice
> from heaven said, 'This is my Son, whom I love; with him I am
> well pleased.'
>   *Then* Jesus was led by the Spirit into the desert to be tempted
> by the devil [italics mine].

The normal pattern of spiritual experience is that a time of special blessing is followed by a period of testing. After the dove, the devil. After the blessing, the battle. In this Jesus was no exception. Mark in his Gospel emphasizes this point by his use of the words 'at once' (1:12).

Scarcely had the reassuring voice from heaven died away than the Lord found Himself in stern confrontation with His arch-enemy. Had the Father confirmed Christ's divine Sonship? Then the devil will focus his assaults on that very point with his twice-repeated insinuation: 'If you are the Son of God. . . .'

The locale of the temptation

According to generally accepted tradition, the scene of Christ's epic encounter with Satan was a desolate part of the desert of Judea, just north-west of Jericho, known from the time of the Crusades as Mount Quarantania. In stark contrast to the experience of the first Adam, the setting was not a lush garden but an arid desert, where conditions were anything but congenial. The area has been described as a wild tract, rugged and barren, the haunt of fierce wild beasts and even fiercer bandits who, by their deeds of violence, had caused the steep road from Jericho to Jerusalem to be called 'the ascent of blood'.

The evangelists make it clear that the initiative in the Temptation did not lie with the devil. In this, as in every other part of the plan of redemption, the initiative is with God. Each of the Synoptic Gospels stresses the initiative of the Holy Spirit in this event:

Jesus was led *by the Spirit* into the desert to be tempted by the devil (Mt 4:1).

At once *the Spirit* sent him out into the desert, and he was in the desert forty days, being tempted by Satan (Mk 1:12–13).

Jesus, full of *the Holy Spirit*, returned from the Jordan and was led by the Spirit in the desert, where for forty days he was tempted by the devil (Lk 4:1·2, italics mine).

From this stern ministry of the Spirit, we learn that the Temptation was no unimportant incident, but an integral and significant part of God's plan of redemption. Just as Christ's death was part of 'God's set purpose and fore-knowledge' (Acts 2:23), so there was a divine necessity for this encounter in the desert, and Jesus obediently entered upon it at the direct instigation of the Holy Spirit.

Since none of His disciples were with Him in the desert, from what source did the evangelists obtain their detailed knowledge of the Temptation? The answer must surely be that it is autobiographical. During one of those sacred private sessions when Jesus opened His heart to His friends, He must have told them the story.

Personal devil or impersonal evil?

In his weighty book, *The Days of His Flesh*, David Smith expounds this event without any mention of the devil what-soever. The temptations that came to Jesus are represented as coming from within His personality. For example: 'He questioned within himself', 'There arose before him a vision', 'His thoughts turned to the holy city'.[2]

But such a treatment is not true to the explicit statements of Scripture. It is eisegesis rather than exegesis. Compare the above statements with the following: 'The tempter came to him and said . . . The devil took him to the holy city . . . Jesus said to him . . .' (Mt 4:3, 5, 10). Also: 'When the devil had finished all this tempting, he left him until an opportune time' (Lk 4:13).

If words have any real meaning, it is surely quite im-possible to fit this language into the concept of the mere personification of evil, for this would cast Jesus in the role of being His own tempter! Only a real confrontation of real personalities will fit the case.

If Jesus did not confront a personal, factual devil as the records assert, the only alternative is that in the desert He was engaged in an inner conflict with His own desires and ambitions, and His temptations thus originated in His own personality.

But the Scriptures expressly exclude any thought of there being any disposition to evil in His Holy Person—'In him was no sin.' Further, Jesus expressly negated any possession of a sinful nature or tendencies when He said, 'The prince of this world is coming. He has no hold on me' (Jn 14:30). And again, 'Can any of you prove me guilty of sin?' (Jn 8:46). The sinless Christ was conscious that there was no traitor in His breast.

In these days of burgeoning occultism and blatant satanism, it is much easier for people to believe the biblical references to the devil than it was two or three decades ago.

> Not alone in pain and gloom
> Does the abhorred tempter come;
> Not alone in light and pleasure
> Proffers he poisoned measure;
> When the soul doth rise
> Nearest to its native skies,
> There the exalted spirit finds
> Borne upon the heavenly winds,
> Satan in an angel's guise
> With voice divine and innocent eyes.
>   *Richard W. Gilder*

The Temptation was really a series of attacks and solicitations that continued for forty days. And this was only the first engagement in a protracted campaign. Indeed, Jesus was tempted right throughout His life.

But in this special crisis the attack focused upon His being the Son of God, the Messiah, the Representative Head of a new humanity. This is implicit in the statement that the devil left Jesus until an opportune time. The period of the Temptation is significant, as 'forty' is one of the mystical numbers of Scripture, and is usually regarded as the number of trial and testing.

In sending a message of comfort to Sister Katherine Hustwhat in her trial, John Bunyan's church referred to her Lord's Temptation in these words:

> Stirre up the grace of God that is in thee, and lay hold by faith on eternal life; and count when thou art tempted much, yet the end of the temptation will come. And remember that even our dearest Lord could not breake off the tempter in ye middle. But when Sathan had ended all the temptation, then he departed from Him for a season.

Could Christ have sinned?

This question inevitably arises in any consideration of the Temptation; a question on which divergent views have been held by equally godly and competent scholars in all ages. Since it involves the mystery of the union in Christ's single Personality of a divine and a human nature, it may be that we must await the eternal day to receive the authoritative answer, for the negative and positive views can each be argued with considerable plausibility. The important common factor in both views is, of course, that all are agreed that Christ *did not* sin. But a division of opinion arises immediately it is asserted that He *could not* sin.

On the one hand it is argued that the thought of a temptation where there is no possibility of yielding to it seems to be academic and unreal. It is affirmed that this would take the incident out of line with the Eden temptation, and would greatly diminish its power of appeal to the tempted soul. It is contended that it would not be logically possible for the New Testament writers to refer to our Lord's temptation as a ground of confidence for the believers overcoming theirs by His sympathetic help (Heb 2:18; 4:14–16). It would mean that His humanity would be essentially different from our own, and that He would enjoy an incredible advantage over tempted humanity.[3]

The case is stated by Philip Schaff:

> Had He been endowed from the start with absolute impeccability, or the impossibility of sinning, He could not be a true man, or our model for imitation . . . Freedom implies the power of choice between good and evil, and the power of disobedience as well as of obedience to the law of God.[4]

On the other hand, it is argued that the implications of the suggestion that Christ could have sinned are stupendous. We would be faced with the almost inconceivable position that His human nature could act in opposition to His holy divine nature, a possibility that would negate the essential unity of His Person. He was not two persons but one, and these natures could never be separated after He became incarnate.

Since both natures were indissolubly united in Him, if He could sin, then God could sin, for He claimed absolute identity with God—a possibility that seems intolerable. Since Scripture affirms that Christ is the same yesterday, today and for ever, it would follow that if He could have sinned yesterday, then He can sin today—a shaky foundation, surely, for the work of redemption.

Whichever view is embraced, certain facts emerge:

1. *Christ did not sin* in thought, word or deed.

2. Scripture draws no exact parallel between Adam and Christ, or between Adam's temptation and His, although there are some common factors. Christ's human nature is referred to as 'the holy one to be born'—a unique expression—and is attributed to the Holy Spirit coming upon Mary, and the power of the Most High overshadowing her (Lk 1:35). No such assertions were made concerning the first Adam.

3. Our Lord's temptations were painfully real tempta-

tions. His participation in our human nature was so complete that the seductions of the devil made a strong appeal to Him. It was no mere theatrical display or shadow boxing.

4. It involved Him in deep suffering. 'He himself suffered when he was tempted' (Heb 2:18). Close contact with sin was so repugnant to His pure and sensitive nature that it caused Him the keenest pain. My father could never hear a musical discord without sharply drawing in his breath. How much more would the discord of sin pain our sensitive Lord.

The conflict in the desert was so intense that for forty days food had no meaning to the Lord. It was only after the battle was over that He became famished. Later, when the devil renewed his attack in the Garden of Gethsemane, the conflict was so fierce, the temptation so real and the suffering so intense, that blood-sweat forced its way through His pores. The testing was acute, the suffering real.

5. It can be argued that the suffering is most poignant, not to those who yield to the temptation, but to those who resist it to the end and do not sin.

> Sympathy with the sinner in his trial [wrote Bishop Westcott], does not depend on the experience of sin, but on the strength of the temptation to sin which only the sinless can know in its full intensity. He who falls, yields before the last strain. Jesus experienced the violence of the attacks of temptation as no others, because all others are sinful, and therefore not able to remain standing until the temptations have exhausted all their terrible violence on them.[5]

To me personally, in spite of the very real problems that admittedly are involved, the thought that Christ could be implicated in sins of His own originating seems totally unacceptable. Surely the solution to the complex problem must lie elsewhere. I am content to accept the revealed facts that although Jesus suffered acutely in desperately real temptations, He did not sin, but emerged from the ordeal unsullied and unstained. Because of this triumph 'He is able to help those who are being tempted' (Heb 2:18). The full explanation must await the coming day of fuller knowledge.

The threefold temptation

The purpose of our Lord's testing in the desert was not to see whether He would sin, but to prove His sinlessness, and therefore His qualification to be the substitute for those who were not sinless.

The three temptations were representative as well as personal. He entered the battle on our behalf, and was tempted in His representative role as Son of Man.

In essence, the temptations covered the whole range of human desire, for ultimately all human desires find expression in three main channels. It is in this sense that we can understand the statement: 'We do not have a high priest who is unable to sympathise with our weaknesses, but we have one who has been tempted in every way, just as we are' (Heb 4:15).

The three temptations assailed the Lord in the realms of physical need, spiritual trust and divine mission. They also correspond to John's analysis of 'all that is in the world, the lust of the flesh, and the lust of the eyes, and the pride of life' (1 Jn 2:16, Authorized Version).

The parallels between the Eden and the desert temptations are close, and the same essential elements appear in each. Take first the Eden temptation:

'The lust of the flesh'—*appetite*—'good for food'.
'The lust of the eyes'—*avarice*—'a delight to the eyes'.
'The pride of life'—*ambition*—'desirable to make one wise'.

Bring alongside this the desert temptation:

'The lust of the flesh'—*appetite*—'command stones to become bread'.

'The lust of the eyes'—*avarice*—'all kingdoms of the world'.

'The pride of life'—*ambition*—'cast yourself down'.

On the surface the devil's seductions seemed legitimate and innocuous, but in each there was a skilfully concealed hook. Each temptation involved an incitement to act in self-interest and in independence of His Father, and without reference to His will. This He would not do.

> Thus one by one the current ideas of what the Messiah should do are reviewed and rejected: bribery by material prosperity; bread; alliance with the world's own forces to subdue the world; the spectacle of signs and wonders.[6]

One of the most helpful features for us failing men in the whole drama, lies in the manner in which Jesus gained the victory. Satan incited Him to draw on His power as Son of God, but as Campbell Morgan said:

> He declined to use the prerogatives and powers of deity in any other way than was possible to any other man. He did not face temptation or overcome it in the realm of His deity, but in the magnificence of His manhood, tested for thirty years in ordinary private life, and for forty days in the loneliness of the desert. Jesus was in the desert as man's representative.

Had He used His divine powers to gratify His desires by a miracle, He would have forfeited His power to appeal to us men who possess no such powers.

The method of victory

In the heat of the conflict, Jesus three times unsheathed 'the sword of the Spirit which is the Word of God', and took the offensive against His adversary. The whole event affords incidental insight into His view of the Scriptures. To Him the dictum of Scripture was authoritative and final and it possessed divine power. It is ironical that in all three cases the passages Jesus selected to repel the tempter were taken from the Book of Deuteronomy, the book which more than any other has been the object of destructive criticism.

There were two notable elements in His victory over the devil that have special relevance for us in our battle with temptation.

1. He constantly yielded the sovereign control of His whole being to the Holy Spirit, for this is in essence what it means to be filled with the Spirit. The result was that after He had met and defeated His enemy, 'Jesus returned into Galilee in the power of the Spirit' (Lk 4:14), enriched by the conflict, and continued His ministry through the Spirit's enabling 'after giving instructions through the Holy Spirit to the apostles' (Acts 1:2).

2. He implicitly accepted the authority of the Word of God, and obeyed it without reservation, mental or otherwise. Consequently the Spirit was able to recall to His mind at the critical moment the Scripture that exactly suited the situation and exposed the hidden hook. His spoken word carried with it the power and authority of God. Jesus did not argue with Satan, He just asserted the affirmations of Scripture, and for them Satan had no answer. *The same Holy Spirit* is willing to perform the same office for us in our time of need. Are our minds sufficiently well stored for Him to recall the appropriate Scripture when we need it?

Does not the fact of our Lord having suffered temptations that are common to all bring Him very near to us? It imparts assurance that He understands and cares. It will stimulate our fellowship as we walk in deeper dependence on Him.

> 'Tempted and tried!'
> O the terrible tide
> May be raging and deep, may be wrathful and wide,
>   Yet its fury is vain,

For the Lord shall restrain
And forever and ever Jehovah shall reign.

'Tempted and tried!'
There is One at my side
And never in vain shall His children confide,
He shall save and defend,
For He loves to the end,
Adorable Master, and glorious Friend.

F. R. Havergal

History was repeating itself. Corruption had invaded the holy place of God's habitation, not simply in the form of grasping commercialism, but more importantly in terms of robbing God by desecrating His abode . . . Bad as the merchandising was, this in itself was not the major complaint. It is rather this, that by turning the court into a mart of trade, the Jewish authorities had denied the Gentiles the privilege of using the portion of the temple open to them. They could not go into the interior courts, for this was expressly denied to them. A barrier with warning signs kept them confined to the outer perimeter.[1]

E. F. Harrison

4

The Purpose of Christ's Cleansing
of the Temple

When it was almost time for the Jewish Passover, Jesus went up to Jerusalem. In the temple courts he found men selling cattle, sheep and doves, and others sitting at tables exchanging money. So he made a whip out of cords, and drove all from the temple area, both sheep and cattle; he scattered the coins of the money-changers and overturned their tables. To those who sold doves he said, 'Get these out of here! *How dare you turn my Father's house into a market!'* (Jn 2: 13–16, italics mine).

Jesus entered the temple area and drove out all who were buying and selling there. He overturned the tables of the money-changers and the benches of those selling doves. 'It is written,' he said to them, *'My house will be called a house of prayer, but you are making it a "den of robbers" '* (Mt 21: 12–13, italics mine).

On first appearances this astounding incident in the life of our Lord seems quite out of keeping with the common conception of Him. It is certainly not what one would have expected of Him. Probably popular thought among those of the older generation has been influenced more than is realized by the children's hymn 'Gentle Jesus Meek and Mild'.

In this incident Jesus was anything but mild. His drastic action indicated the depth of His feeling, and revealed the importance He attached to this bizarre event.

Christ's 'cleansing of the temple', as it is called, was an historical act with profound spiritual significance, for it reveals a side of His character which reflects God's anger and implacable hostility to sin, whether it be moral or spiritual. It was not an isolated act, for two cleansings are recorded—as if to indicate a continuing activity in His Church. He is continually at work exposing and expelling the evil and maintaining its purity.

The incident recorded by John appears to have occurred at the beginning of the Lord's ministry, and the accounts recorded in the Synoptic Gospels, at the end. Many expositors have considered that there may have been only one cleansing, and that the records have become confused, but a careful comparison of the two accounts does not reveal any such necessary confusion. No satisfying explanation has been given why Jesus should not have repeated His action.

Leon Morris has demonstrated striking differences between the accounts in John's Gospel and those of the Synoptics—differences that are easily reconcilable if there were two cleansings, but are perplexing if there was only one.

John's record is quite different from that of Matthew in setting, tone and words employed. If it be asked why there should be two such similar cleansings, there is a simple and natural explanation—*evil has a remarkable capacity for revival!* As they were protected by the temple police, the mercenary priests and traders doubtless returned the next day having recovered from the humiliating shock of the Lord's drastic action. It would not take long for them to revert to their former sacrilegious practices.

When they returned, the profaning of the temple apparently became more flagrant than ever, and Jesus reproved them in even sterner terms than on the previous occasion. The 'market' of John's record becomes 'a den of robbers' in that of Matthew. It was God's declared intention that the temple should be 'a house of prayer for all nations', but they had turned it into a thieves' kitchen, or as C.K. Barrett translates it 'a nationalist stronghold', from which the Gentiles were excluded. 'For this profitable monopoly the priestly families took possession of the one place in Jerusalem where a Gentile or a stranger was permitted to say his prayers.'

These two incidents hold a solemn contemporary lesson for us all. When under the conviction of the Holy Spirit we expel evil from our lives, but later go back on our renunciation and again embrace it, it returns with even greater enslaving power.

The symbolism of the temple

The temple held a unique place in the national life of Israel. It was a magnificent building, and was held in higher esteem than even the King's palace. It was the focal point of the nation's distinctive sacrificial system. The worshippers gloried in the beauty of its architecture. 'As he was leaving the temple, one of his disciples said to him, 'Look, Teacher! What massive stones! What magnificent buildings!' (Mk 13:1).

Of the two Greek words for 'temple', one was used of the central shrine which could be used only by the priests. The other word, which occurs here, refers to the whole precincts of the temple. It comprised several courts: the court of the Gentiles; the court of the Israelites; the holy place; the holy of holies.

Each year vast crowds gathered for the Feast of the Passover, but the corrupt and avaricious priests had turned the court of the Gentiles into a sordid trading-post, and thus excluded them from worshipping the true God. Instead of the voice of prayer there was the lowing of cattle and the bargaining of covetous traders.

The temple filled an important role, not only in the nation but in the purpose of God. He planned it as the meeting place on earth between man and Himself. Instead of becoming the centre of the world's religion, it had now been desecrated and degraded until it was no more than a robbers' den. The building retained its original magnificence, but God is more interested in inward purity than in outward beauty. Men are more important than stones and mortar. The abuses introduced by the priests had entirely frustrated God's plan of blessing for the world, and His disapproval must find expression.

The symbolism of the temple is carried over into the New Testament era. In addressing the Corinthian Christians, Paul said:

> Don't you know that you yourselves are God's temple and that God's Spirit lives in you? If anyone destroys God's temple, God will destroy him; for God's temple is sacred, and you are that temple (1 Cor 3:16-17).

> Do you not know that your body is a temple of the Holy Spirit, who is in you? (1 Cor 6:19).

This temple, too, can be desecrated and profaned. The spirit of the world can invade Christ's Church. Fleshly thoughts and indulgences can defile the body of the Christian.

The skilful pen of Dr F.B. Meyer draws a parallel between our body and an inn thronged with guests. It can be a library filled with stores of knowledge. It can be a finance house devoted to the making and spending of money. It can be a playhouse devoted to the pursuit of pleasure. It can be a sty in which swinish passions hold sway. Or it can be a temple set apart for the worship and service of God. We ourselves decide which function it will fulfil.

'Christ purged the temple,' said George Herbert. 'So

must thou thy heart.' Paul wrote in the same vein: 'Since we have these promises, dear friends, let us purify ourselves from everything that contaminates body and spirit' (2 Cor 7:1).

The anger of Jesus

It had been prophesied, and the Jews expected that when the Messiah came it would be with a scourge to evildoers in the nation. When at the very beginning of His public ministry Jesus came to the temple with uplifted scourge, the Jews were not slow to interpret this as a Messianic claim, as indeed it was.

The whole incident demonstrates the unique moral authority He possessed and displayed. How could a lone and uninfluential man so thoroughly master that great crowd? Why did He meet no resistance as He drove them out? Why did the temple guards not intervene? Why were the priests and officials silent? Why did the traders not fight for their rights and livelihood? 'In the face of such a mockery of worship, the spirit of Jesus blazed with such fierceness of denunciation that no one dared gainsay him.'

Because Jesus was perennially filled with the Spirit and ablaze with holy zeal for His Father's glory, His moral authority was irresistible. He found an ally in the consciences of those He rebuked. In the Garden of Gethsemane He displayed a similar authority that paralysed the rabble that came to arrest Him: 'When Jesus said, 'I am he,' they drew back and fell to the ground' (Jn 18:6).

The anger of Jesus is not a popular topic and is not often dealt with in contemporary preaching. But this neglected aspect of His character is important, for it is a revelation of the true nature of God. The concept of the wrath of God is no invention of theologians for their own purposes. No one spoke of it more solemnly than did the Lord Himself.

In Matthew's account of the second cleansing, he records

that 'when the chief priests and the teachers of the law saw the wonderful things he did and *the children shouting in the temple area, 'Hosanna to the Son of David,'* they were indignant' (21:15, italics mine).

But Jesus was indignant because they had desecrated His Father's house. Though He was the Prince of Peace, Jesus was no pacifist in the presence of evil. He could not permit evil to go unchallenged. Was this not the explanation of His enigmatic and paradoxical statement 'I did not come to bring peace but a sword'? Where personal injury was involved He would turn the other cheek, but when His Father's interests were in jeopardy and His house profaned, He used an uplifted scourge. Ours is no anaemic Lord.

As Jesus moved towards the traders, the lightning of a holy anger flashed from His eyes. 'The wrath of the Lamb' is a terrifying concept, but in reality righteous anger is no less noble than love. He loved righteousness and hated iniquity with equal intensity.

It was love for the man with the withered hand that moved Him to hot anger against the callous religious leaders who would have denied him healing. It was because of His love for the Gentiles that Jesus was fiercely angry with those who were making it impossible for them to worship God, and incidentally were exploiting their own people.

Jesus was angry, but His anger was *sinless* because it was *selfless*. Our anger is usually sinful because it is self-centred.

The purpose of the cleansing

It was desecration of His Father's house that was the essence of the sin and blasphemy of the hypocritical religious leaders. Jesus made this clear when he put forward this charge: 'It is written, 'My house shall be called a house of prayer, but you are making it a den of robbers' (Mt 21:13). Secularism and materialism had invaded and captured the holy temple of God. The bleating of sheep, lowing of cattle, cooing of doves and clinking of money was drowning the voice of prayer. The whole atmosphere was mercenary and secular. Instead of reverent worship there was heated haggling and cheating. This situation must be changed.

The fact that *the priests themselves had vested interests in the sordid temple trading* was another element of His holy anger. The shops and markets in the temple area were controlled by the high priest Annas and his family, and the priests also shared in their rake-off. The men chosen to be God's representatives, were actively engaged in desecrating His house. There were two elements involved in their operations:

The first perversion was in relation to *the annual sacrifices*. It was much more convenient for a worshipper to buy an animal on the spot than to drag it unwillingly through the crowded streets of Jerusalem to have it inspected for meeting the kosher requirements. But they were being fleeced by unscrupulous traders who charged exorbitant prices for the sacrificial animals. It really amounted to blackmail in the very house of God.

Then there was *the temple tax*. Every Jew over nineteen years of age had to pay a tax of a half-shekel, which was the equivalent of two days' wages. Because 'the shekel of the sanctuary' was the only acceptable currency for this tax, and there were many other currencies in circulation, the Roman money the pilgrims brought had to be exchanged. For this the moneychangers extorted a commission of up to twenty-five per cent. Because of the profit this rake-off brought to their coffers, the religious authorities had tolerated this abuse until Jesus intervened.

The Master was not indifferent to *the social injustice* involved in these illegal transactions. He could not, and did not, ignore the blatant fleecing of the pilgrims who could ill afford the amount demanded. Nor could He tolerate the extortion and blackmail that were defiling His Father's house. He therefore expressed His concern about social justice and pure spiritual worship in a manner that would attract the maximum public notice, and would focus attention on the guilty men. His justified anger burned with a pure and holy flame. His action directly challenged the authority of the high priest because they were there with his authority.

The method of the cleansing

Until Jesus appeared on the scene, the traders and their victims had become so accustomed to prevailing conditions that they resignedly accepted the *status quo*. The callous merchants were so hardened that they had grown unconscious of the incongruity of their actions, and their dupes had abandoned any hope of change.

It may be that we, too, have accepted the *status quo* in our own lives, whereas there may be much unsuspected sin present that must be cleansed before the Holy Spirit can work in us powerfully. With this possibility in mind, it is instructive to note the way in which Jesus dealt with this situation and see if there is any parallel in the temple of our lives.

1. He exposed the evils of the prevalent temple worship and the abuses that had crept in. This is always the first and essential step in the cleansing process. This prayer is always appropriate:

> Throw light into the darkened cells,
> Where passion reigns within,
> Quicken my conscience 'til it feels
> The loathsomeness of sin.
> *F. Bottome*

2. He banished the secular that had ousted the sacred. It

was a clean sweep. 'He made a scourge of cords and drove them all out of the temple.' Wordly standards and practices had become the norm, but Jesus would not allow such a condition to continue. Drastic action was called for.

What an uproar there must have been as Jesus, clothed with irresistible authority, went into action! What scrabbling on the floor as the moneychangers tried to recover the scattered coins! What mutterings and threatenings! What universal consternation!

It might be a salutary exercise to ask ourselves what changes the Lord might have to make in the temple of *our* lives if His highest purpose for us is to be realized. Have we allowed the secular to invade our homes and largely oust the sacred? Would He have to switch off our TV sets on some programmes?

3. He restored divine standards and substituted eternal values for the secondary. First things must come first. Good things may be the enemy of the best. Is a good deal of our time occupied with things which, though legitimate, are of only secondary importance? Do we tend to spend a disproportionate amount of our time on things that are of only passing value, while neglecting the all-important culture of the inner life? He would alter this.

4. He prohibited even small desecrations of the temple. The custom had apparently arisen of using the temple court as a short-cut between the city and the Mount of Olives. But Jesus would not permit even a minor desecration of the sanctuary. 'He would not allow anyone to carry merchandise through the temple' (Mk 11:6). What presumption! But what authority! See Him standing there ordering them back! And this must have continued for some time.

We should ask the Holy Spirit to make us sensitive to small sins or indulgences that would short-circuit spiritual power. Jesus knew that small deviations lead to large divergences.

Christ's consuming zeal

When the awed disciples saw the implacable purpose with which Jesus routed the unsurpers, they were at a loss to understand the change in Him. What had come over Him? Never before had they seen such holy anger. Only afterwards did the explanation dawn on them: 'His disciples remembered that it is written, "Zeal for your house will consume me"' (Jn 2:17). The word 'zeal' carries the idea of 'boiling; bubbling up'. They saw that Jesus was boiling over with the heat of His own passion for His Father's glory and for the blessing of His world.

If we invite the same Lord to cleanse the temple of our lives, must we not expect Him to challenge our secularism and materialistic outlook as He did with the Jews of old? Should we not co-operate with Him in restoring what is primary to its rightful place? Is He more tolerant of our sins today than He was of those of His own day? Malachi prophesied the coming of the Lord to His temple:

> Then suddenly the Lord you are seeking will come to his temple. . . . But who can endure the day of his coming? Who can stand when he appears? (Mal 3:1-2).

For the traders and priests, that momentous day had begun as usual. They never dreamed that a great crisis lay just ahead, and were staggered when the Lord came 'suddenly to His temple'. As the prophet had foretold, they were not able to stand before Him when He appeared.

We may have begun this day as usual, never dreaming that the Lord might suddenly come to His temple. Let us listen to His voice. Let us welcome Him into our lives to purify them, and fit them for His service. The prophet indicates the method He adopts to achieve this end:

> He will sit as a refiner and purifier of silver; he will purify the Levites and refine them like gold and silver. Then the Lord will have men who will bring offerings in righteousness, and the

offerings of Judah and Jerusalem will be acceptable to the Lord
(Mal 3:3).

Though the Transfiguration is one of the most astonishing of all the experiences of our Lord while on earth, for no adequate reason (we would not say without any reason) it has not been given in Christological literature, and most emphatically in apologetic literature, the consideration to which it is entitled. Professor Bruce opens his excellent chapter on this subject exclaiming:

'The transfiguration is one of those passages in the Saviour's earthly history which an expositor would rather pass over in reverent silence. . . . Who is able fully to speak of that wondrous night-scene among the mountains, during which heaven was for a few brief minutes let down to earth, and the mortal body of Jesus shone with celestial brightness? It is too high for us, this august spectacle, we cannot attain to it; its grandeur oppresses and stupefies; its mystery surpasses our comprehension; its glory is ineffable.'[1]

Wilbur M. Smith

5
The Purpose of Christ's Transfiguration

There he was transfigured before them. His face shone like the sun, and his clothes became as white as the light (Mt 17:2).

There he was transfigured before them. His clothes became dazzling white, whiter than anyone in the world could bleach them (Mk 9:2-3).

As he was praying, the appearance of his face changed, and his clothes became as bright as a flash of lightning (Lk 9:29).

The three complementary accounts in the Synoptic Gospels of the transfiguration of our Lord, admit us into one of the most remarkable and mysterious incidents of His earthly life. So unique and astonishing is it, that one is at a loss to understand the reason for its comparative neglect in both the written and the spoken ministry of the Church. Perhaps the diffidence referred to at the opening of the chapter is the explanation.

It will be noted that each of the Gospel writers highlights a different facet of the event—'white as the light' 'dazzling white' 'as bright as a flash of lightning'.

The transfiguration experience was unique in that it was the only occasion in Christ's earthly life when the blaze of

His inherent glory and majesty was permitted to flash forth. Another unusual feature was that two men, both of whose earthly lives had come to an end centuries before, held conversation with Him on the mountain.

> Rays of glory found their way
> Through the garment of decay,
> With which as a cloak He had
> His divinest splendour clad.
> *R. Chenevix Trench*

The historicity of the alleged incident has been doubted, but there are strong reasons for accepting it as an authentic fact. The details of the three Gospel records are remarkably harmonious. The surrounding events are undoubtedly historical. The narratives bear all the marks of reality, and one cannot read them without being impressed with the outward actuality of the scene. The suggestion that Jesus experienced an ecstatic, perhaps glossalalic, vision later interpreted by His disciples is not convincing; nor is the view that the story is a misplaced resurrection narrative.

For those to whom the Scriptures are the final authority the testimony of Peter is conclusive.

> We did not follow cleverly invented stories when we told you about the power and coming of our Lord Jesus Christ, but *we were eye witnesses of his majesty.* For he received honour and glory from God the Father when the voice came from the Majestic Glory, saying, 'This is my Son, whom I love; with him I am well pleased.' *We ourselves heard this voice that came from heaven when we were with him on the sacred mountain* (2 Pet 1:16-18, italics mine).

Scholars are at variance as to the exact location of this nocturnal scene. Mount Tabor was the generally accepted spot, but as it was only 1900 feet high and not the 'high mountain' of Mark, it has been bypassed in favour of Mount Hermon which is 9000 feet high. The fact that Mount Tabor was crowned with a fortified city would hardly make it the most suitable place for such a manifestation. Another possibility is Mount Miron (3926 feet), the highest mountain within Israel.

The fact that Jesus took only the trusted three of His intimate friends with Him, and His charge to them to maintain silence afterwards, would indicate the greatness of the privilege they enjoyed. As the incident gave evidence of the Lord's Messianic claim, He obviously feared that unguarded talk might incite premature Messianic excitement.

The selection of this inner circle of three for the sacred occasion was not a matter of favouritism. He chose them because, more than the others, they were spiritually responsive and willing to pay the price of close following. And are we not all, like them, as intimate with the Lord as we have chosen to be?

The relevance of this event to the life and experience of twentieth-century Christians may not be immediately evident. The accompanying splendour seems to remove it from the everyday life and spiritual problems of ordinary men. But if we probe beneath the surface, we will discover that there is a divine and beneficent purpose in the mysterious incident that has a very blessed meaning for us.

The purpose for Christ

Christ's true humanity involved Him in a real identity with the sinless infirmities of our human nature. The very fact that He wished to have His three friends with Him on this occasion evidenced His appreciation of congenial human companionship. In the midst of the drabness and difficulty of His life on earth, the momentary suffusion and outshining of the familiar majesty and glory must have meant a great deal to Him.

Taken together, Peter's great and comforting confession of the Lord's divine Sonship (Mt 16:16), and the confirming voice of His Father, 'This is my Son, whom I love; with him

I am well pleased,' must have been a fresh source of strength and inspiration as He trod the way of the cross.

He had shared with His friends His impending death, and now two visitors from the other world, Moses and Elijah, had come to converse with Him about 'his departure [lit. exodus], which he was about to bring to fulfilment at Jerusalem' (Lk 9:31).

The voice from heaven was no mere subjective phenomenon. Peter plainly stated, 'We ourselves heard this voice that came from heaven when we were with him on the sacred mountain' (2 Pet 1:18). The same voice had spoken at His baptism in Jordan, but a fresh assurance of divine approval coming at this crisis in His ministry would have been greatly treasured. It no doubt strengthened and nerved Him for the dread ordeal ahead. It was a foretaste of 'the joy set before him'. Men may malign and misunderstand Him, but that mattered less when He knew that He was approved and understood in heaven.

Dr G. Campbell Morgan held that this incident attested the attainment of the perfection in Christ's manhood that conferred on Him the right to enter heaven. 'Here at last that humanity, perfect in creation, perfect through probation, was perfected in glory.'[2]

The purpose for the disciples

For them, too, the experience held deep significance. The fact that they honoured the Lord's instruction: 'Don't tell anyone what you have seen, until the Son of Man has been raised from the dead,' is eloquent of the awe which the vision had engendered in them.

The whole scene was staged 'before them'—that is, for their benefit. The voice from heaven had a message for them as well as for their Master. The authoritative command was to 'listen to Him!'—in the sense of heeding and obeying Him. Only a few days before, Peter had had the temerity to dispute with the Master. He had to heed and obey.

To the disciples, the transfiguration scene came as confirmation of Christ's unwelcome prediction of His approaching death at Jerusalem. In those dark days the memory of the vision would somewhat soften for them the sufferings that lay ahead. Also, Christ's essential deity was so convincingly displayed before their eyes as to render doubt impossible. Moses and Elijah, the two chosen representatives of Judaism, interpreted to them the purpose of His mission. The very presence of these patriarchs would have been to the disciples a pledge and assurance of their own immortality. Here was tangible evidence that the grave was not the end.

The Lord had promised that He would come again in glory, and they were now being given a foretaste of that glory.

The glory of the Son

'We have seen his glory, the glory of the one and only Son, who came from the Father, full of grace and truth,' recalls John (1:14). By the expressions the other three evangelists use to convey an adequate impression of the glory of their transfigured Lord, it seems almost as though they are competing with one another in their eagerness to convey something of the splendour of the scene.

Matthew says: 'His face shone like the sun, and his clothes became as white as the light' (17:2). Mark adds his description, 'His clothes became dazzling white' (9:3). Luke contributes another element: 'The appearance of his face changed, and his clothes became as bright as a flash of lightning' (9:29).

> His raiment white and glistening
> White as the glistening snow;
> His form a blaze of splendour,

The like no sun can show;
His wondrous eyes resplendent
In ecstasy of prayer;
His radiant face transfigured
To heaven's own beauty there.

George Rawson

Our word 'metamorphosis' is derived from the Greek word translated 'transfiguration'. It means 'a change into another form', and that is precisely what happened on this occasion. Taking the records at their face value, it seems clear that there was some *physical* change in our Lord's body. It says plainly that He was transfigured and His disciples saw, and later commented on, the change. It was not only that His clothes were irradiated with an unearthly glory.

The cumulative effect of the expressions used, is to present the impression of unequalled majesty and glory. It was not *external* illumination as from a spotlight. Nor was it mere *reflected* glory as in the case of Moses when he descended from Mount Sinai. The shining of His face was the result of prolonged communion with God.

The disciples saw the change in their Master take place before their very eyes. Christ's inner radiance, *His inherent glory,* gradually irradiated His garments which became translucent and gleaming with the whiteness of pure light. Common to each of the three narratives are the two features of dazzling whiteness and blazing light—a light that did not have its source on earth. If we combine the records, we are presented with the majesty of the Person of the Lord. No wonder Peter wanted to perpetuate the experience!

We can only conclude that the transfiguration was not glory falling on Him from some external source, but the flashing forth of His own inherent glory which, though always there, was concealed by the veil of flesh.

Is it without significance for us that it was 'while He was

praying' that the appearance of His face became different? Prolonged communion with God will always transfigure. 'Why is it that so little of this radiance caught from heaven shines from us?' askes Alexander Maclaren. 'There is but one answer. It is because our communion with God is so infrequent, hurried and superficial.'[3]

The glory of His cross

'Moses and Elijah . . . spoke about his departure [exodus], which he was about to bring to fulfilment at Jerusalem' (Lk 9:30-31).

Various reasons have been given for the appearance of these two patriarchs with Christ at the sacred rendezvous on the mountain. Why these two? Was it because of the distinctive nature of their departure from this life that they were chosen to speak with the Lord concerning His impending exodus? More probably it was because they were the acknowledged representatives of the law and the prophets. Moses represented the law, Elijah the prophets, but Jesus, grace.

A rabbinic legend has it that Moses died by a kiss from the mouth of God. Elijah was translated into heaven to the accompaniment of a whirlwind and a chariot of fire. These two heavenly ambassadors, commissioned by the Father to converse with the Son concerning His approaching exodus from earth, and to assure Him of heaven's continuing interest, surrendered to Him their seals of office as the representatives of Judaism.

The disciples were well-versed in the Scriptures so they could hardly fail to link Christ's 'exodus' with that which Moses began in the desert, but had been powerless to carry to completion. The vision of His glory would assure them that, as their heavenly Joshua, He would lead His people triumphantly into the heavenly Canaan.

As the three men listened in to heaven's conversation,

they were able to see Christ's impending death from heaven's viewpoint, and not merely from that of their own personal loss. They gained fresh insight into the scope of God's eternal purpose. They saw their Master's death not only as something He was to suffer, but as a glorious victory He would accomplish (Lk 9:31).

We too need a new and deeper view of the centrality and cruciality of the cross in the divine programme.

The glory of His power and coming

Peter vividly recalls the transfiguration scene with keen spiritual insight and under the inspiration of the Spirit, and discerns a preview of Christ's second advent:

> We did not follow cleverly invented stories when we told you about the power and coming of our Lord Jesus Christ, but we were eye-witnesses of his majesty (2 Pet 1:16).

Six days before the transfiguration Jesus had been speaking to the multitudes about His coming 'in his Father's glory with the holy angels' (Mk 8:38). He followed on with this enigmatic statement:

> I tell you the truth, some who are standing here will not taste death before they see the Son of Man coming in his kingdom (Mt 16:28).

What was the meaning of these cryptic words? They have been variously explained, but it was doubtless a fore-shadowing of the establishment and progress of the kingdom of Christ. Could there be, in miniature, a more satisfying picture of the main elements of His second advent?

How will He come? Just as He appeared on the mountain: 'in power and great glory', 'He shall come with clouds', 'He shall come in his own glory'.

Who will meet Him at His coming? Those of whom

Moses was representative—the dead in Christ. Those of whom *Elijah* was representative—those who are translated at His coming and never see death.

We who are still alive and are left will be caught up with them in the clouds to meet the Lord in the air. And so we will be with the Lord for ever (1 Thess 4:17).

Moses and Elijah departed. The voice from heaven was silent. The cloud disappeared. 'They saw no-one except Jesus.' But in the transfiguration scene, had they not witnessed a microcosm of the kingdom that Christ will establish when He returns to reign in glory?

> Soon passed that scene of grandeur,
>   But steadfast, changeless, sure,
> Our blest transfiguration
>   Is promised to endure,
> The manifested glory
>   Of our great Lord to see,
> Shall change us to His likeness;
>   As He is, we shall be.
>   *George Rawson*

It remains to be said that Peter's suggestion that they remain on the mountain, isolated from the world's woes below, is no more valid for the Church today than it was for them. Like their Master, they must descend to the tormented, problem-ridden world.

Reginald E.O. White writes:

Raphael's great painting of the Transfiguration divides the canvas almost equally between the rapturous vision on the mountain and the violence and frustration in the valley. There nine disciples were confronted with a tortured epileptic boy, and could not heal him. Below, Raphael seems to say, all is argument, hostility, accusation, failure; above all is light and majesty, power and glory . . . Christian disciples cannot remain, as Peter proposed to do, for ever on the mountain, cosily withdrawn from all life's harsher duties. *They must come down*, become involved in the problem-ridden, pain-racked world. Yet they will not be of saving use unless the vision of the Christ remains still clear in their hearts.[4]

Jesus suffered under Pontius Pilate, was crucified, dead and buried; He descended into hell.

Thus carefully does the church define and jealously defend her faith in Calvary. This emphasis on the passion is certainly less central in modern Christianity than once it was. Such concentration on the darker side of life is distasteful to modern feeling, incomprehensible to modern minds, repulsive to modern pride. For we moderns choose to live in dream worlds of fiction, glamour, wealth, ease, romance and happy endings.

The Church has ever been more realistic and more truthful. Suffering, sin, fear, mortality and despair lurk not far below the surface even of modern hearts; and for such needs there is a message of a Saviour who has gone the whole way through identifying Himself with man. From the centre of His agony, from the very darkness of His tomb, He offers life, and peace and hope.[1]

> *A Christless cross no refuge were for me;*
> *A crossless Christ—no Saviour would He be;*
> *But, O, Christ crucified, I rest in Thee.*
> *Reginald E.O. White*

6

The Purpose of Christ's Death

For this very reason, Christ died and returned to life so that he
might be the Lord of both the dead and the living (Rom 14:9).

Like an ellipse, the Christian faith revolves around twin
centres—two stupendous but well-attested historical
events—Calvary and Pentecost. Standing by itself, either
event would have proved sterile so far as the redemption of
a world of lost men and women is concerned. Calvary was a
glowing demonstration of the victory of love, and yet without the dynamic supplied by the outpouring of the Spirit on
the Day of Pentecost, it would have been stillborn.

The facts of redemption had been complete for fifty days,
but nothing had happened. It required the Pentecostal
effusion to swing the machinery of redemption into
motion, for Pentecost was the necessary complement of
Calvary. The descent and subsequent working of the Holy
Spirit, made *actual,* in the lives of those who believed, all
that Christ's atoning death had made *possible.* When these
twin events are apprehended and appropriated, they form
the basis for a well-rounded and satisfying Christian experience.

We will be examining Pentecost in chapter 11. For now, we consider some of the implications of the death of our Lord with special reference to its effects in the personal experience of the Christian.

Viewed *objectively,* Christ's death was as a propitiation for our sins. 'He is the atoning sacrifice [propitiation] for our sins' (1 Jn 2:2). James Packer writes:

> The basic description of the saving death of Christ in the Bible is as a *propitiation,* that is, as that which quenched God's wrath against us by obliterating our sins from His sight. God's wrath is His righteousness reacting against unrighteousness; it shows itself in retributive justice. But Jesus Christ has shielded us from the nightmare prospect of retributive justice by becoming our representative substitute, in obedience to His Father's will, and receiving the wages of sin in our place. . . . Redeeming love and retributive justice joined hands, so to speak, at Calvary.[2]

Viewed *subjectively,* the death of Christ secures five desirable ends in the life of the Christian.

Deliverance from sin

Even though the death of Christ secured for us this incredible blessing, it would have failed in its full purpose had it left us still under the tyranny of sin. It is not enough for the external suppurating sore to be healed over if the internal focus of infection is not dealt with, and its poison continues to circulate in our bloodstream. Thank God, the perfect redemption achieved by our Lord in His mediatorial work on the cross does not leave us in any such tragic condition.

Paul assures us that:

> Jesus Christ . . . gave himself for us *to redeem us from all wickedness* and to purify for himself a people that are his very own, eager to do what is good (Tit 2:14).

He is saying here that the purpose of the atoning death

was both negative and positive. First, it was in order 'to redeem us from all iniquity' (AV). The expression 'gave himself for us' emphasizes the propitiatory character of His death. It was not only that we might be redeemed (bought back), but also that we might be emancipated from the enslaving power of sin.

Peter affirms that the ransom for our deliverance was paid over by our Lord—not in shining silver or yellow gold but in crimson drops of precious blood:

> For you know it was not with perishable things such as silver or gold that you were redeemed from the empty way of life . . . but with the precious blood of Christ, a lamb without blemish or defect (1 Pet 1:18-19).

By His triple victory over sin, death and the devil, He gained for us *potential deliverance* from sin of every kind—'from all wickedness'—whether conscious or unconscious; from subtle sins of the mind as well as from gross and shameful sins of the flesh.

Crisis or process?

If it be asked whether emancipation from sin's tyrannical domination takes place in a moment, or over a period of time; whether it is a crisis or a gradual process, the paradoxical answer would be 'both'! It was with this thought in mind that F.W.H. Myers wrote:

> Let no man think that sudden in a minute
> All is accomplished, and the work is done,
> Though with the earliest dawn thou should'st begin it,
> Scarce were it ended in thy setting sun.

The *crisis* leading to the experience of emancipation from the power of sin often occurs when, conscious of our inability to achieve our own deliverance, we claim our part in the delivering power of the cross of Christ. Then follows the *process* of sanctification, of holy living. The Holy Spirit makes what was potential, actual in our experience. Freedom from sin's slavery continues as we count on Him to apply the power of Christ's cross and resurrection to our lives.

> For we know that our old self was crucified with him so that the body of sin might be rendered powerless, that we should no longer be slaves to sin—because anyone who has died has been freed from sin (Rom 6:6-7).

A photograph is taken in a single flash of exposure. It is a sudden crisis. In a hundredth of a second the image is imprinted on the sensitive film. True, there had been preliminary preparations and adjustments before the picture could be snapped, but the crisis of exposure took only the briefest moment. Although you have taken a picture of, for example, your friend, you will look in vain on the film for any likeness. The film remains blank until the crisis of exposure is followed up by the process of developing and fixing, and that takes time.

If the image on the film is to be perfectly secured and permanently retained, there is no short cut in the process. Developing acids must eat away that part of the film which obscures the face of your friend. By the crisis of exposure, the image was imprinted. By the process of developing, that which obscures the image is progressively removed, and the likeness of your friend gradually emerges.

Our transformation into the likeness of Christ is like this. *The crisis of faith* is often preceded in a person's life by a preparatory period during which the Holy Spirit produces within that person a profound self-dissatisfaction and an acute sense of personal unworthiness accompanied by a longing for emancipation from sin's power. This leads to a resolving of any controversy with God and righting of fractured relationships with their fellow men. Christ is enthroned as Lord of that life.

Once this crisis is over, *the process of sanctification* is accelerated and continues as long as Christ's Lordship is genuinely recognized. In this process, the Holy Spirit progressively removes anything that prevents the image of Christ being more perfectly reflected. He leads us into the experience of which Paul wrote in exultation:

> But thanks be to God that, though you used to be slaves to sin, you wholeheartedly obeyed the form of teaching to which you were entrusted. You *have been set free from sin*, and have become slaves to righteousness (Rom 6:17-18, italics mine).

Dedication to Christ

Such amazing and divine love as that displayed on the cross, demands a worthy reciprocal response. Nothing less than a thorough shifting of life's centre from self to Christ is adequate, and this is what He both desires and deserves from us. Paul unfolds another purpose in the death of our Lord: 'He died for all, *that those who live should no longer live for themselves* but for him who died for them and was raised again' (2 Cor 5:15, italics mine).

The acceptance of Christ's atonement logically means an end to the life in which the old sinful self holds the central place. A new life is imparted that finds its centre and circumference in Another—in Christ. To live for self after receiving the benefits of His costly salvation, is to rob Him of the fruits of His death and passion.

Christ's love for His children is so palpably sacrificial and disinterested, that it is impossible to conceive of Him taking advantage of us if we concede to Him sovereignty over our lives. And He had nothing less than this in view when He went to the cross: 'For this very reason, Christ died and returned to life so *that he might be the Lord* of both the dead and the living' (Rom 14:9, italics mine).

In these two passages of Scripture, life is viewed in two dimensions—'hitherto' and 'henceforth'. *Hitherto,* self has been central, the chief point of reference. Self-pleasing, self-culture, self-gratification and self-will have been the key words. But the crisis of the cross changes all that. There was an old Indian chief who, on seeing the implications of Christ's death, exclaimed, with rare spiritual insight, 'The cross of Christ condemns me to become a Christian.'

This leads on to *henceforth*. Life is to be 'henceforth unto him', since He died that we should no longer live for ourselves but for Him. Henceforth, time, talents, possessions, friendships, plans and recreations are to be placed directly under His control. The test question for doubtful things will henceforth be, not: 'What is wrong with that anyway?', but, 'Can I do this to the glory of my Lord?'

Contrary to popular expectation, such an embracing of the cross, such a complete surrender and dedication to Christ the Lord, brings a liberty that can be experienced in no other way. We prove that the will of God is not only good and perfect, but also pleasing (Rom 12:2).

The startling truth, that the cross of Christ imposes on the Christian the obligation to live a life of consecration, dawned on Charles T. Studd, founder of the Worldwide Evangelization Crusade, early in his Christian life. He had known about Jesus dying for him, but he had never understood that he did not belong to himself. Redemption, he learned, meant 'buying back', so if he belonged to Christ either he had to be a thief and keep what was not his, or else he had to give up everything to Him. When he came to really appreciate the fact that Jesus Christ had actually died for him, he did not find it hard to give up all in return.

It was this conviction that gave birth to his famous motto: 'If Jesus Christ be God and died for me, then no sacrifice can be too great for me to make for Him.'

Detachment from the world

> The Lord Jesus Christ . . . gave himself for our sins *to rescue us from the present evil age,* according to the will of our God and Father (Gal 1:4, italics mine).

This verse clearly asserts that our Lord's death was not primarily an example of heroism, or merely an expression of love, although it was both. It was essentially a sacrifice for sins—our sins. But it also had a subsidiary purpose—rescuing us from the power and corrupting influence of this present evil world or age. Its purpose was not only to procure our forgiveness, but that once forgiven we should live the life of the age to come.

Paul uses the word 'age' here to refer to the world viewed from the standpoint of time and change, an evil era that is hurrying to its close, and in which there is nothing of eternal value. Jesus entertained the same view of this world as Paul expresses. He warned His men: 'If the world hates you, keep in mind that it hated me first' (Jn 15:18). He told them that if they followed Him closely, they could expect to share the implacable hatred that the world exhibited towards Him.

But Jesus had more in mind than *physical* deliverance from this evil age, for he prayed: 'My prayer is not that you take them out of the world but that you protect them from the evil one' (Jn 17:15). While in the world *physically,* His followers must detach themselves from it *morally and spiritually,* but it must be a separation of insulation, not of isolation.

When on earth, the Lord Himself set an example in this respect, for He was 'separate from sinners' even while eating and drinking with them. It is God's intention that Christians should mix with worldly people, and not isolate themselves in a 'holy ghetto' as they so often do.

He taught that believers are 'the salt of the earth', but salt can only exercise its antiseptic and pungent influence where there is contact. While the believer is in the world, he is not to be of the world. By Christ's death he is rescued from bondage to the standards and the atmosphere of this evil age. His separation is to be like that of the bridegroom, not of the monk—a separation of love that precludes any rival.

Only when we can say with Paul, 'The world has been crucified to me, and I to the world,' do we make our greatest impact upon it. Compromise with the spirit of the age short-circuits the power of the Holy Spirit and neutralizes our spiritual influence. It has been wisely said that he who would do anything for the world must have nothing to do with it.

Continuous communion with Christ

Fellowship with Christ is the highest privilege to which man can aspire. As a result of His death, every believer is privileged to enjoy this communion both in this life and the life to come. Even death cannot interrupt it Paul assures us: 'Our Lord Jesus Christ . . . died for us so that whether we are awake or asleep, we may live together with him' (1 Thess 5:10).

Love can endure anything except distance, and Christ went to the cross in order to annihilate the distance between man and God. It was Charles H. Spurgeon's testimony that for many years there had not been a period of fifteen minutes when he had not been conscious of being in communion with God.

When on her deathbed, Mrs J. Hudson Taylor said to her husband, 'You know, darling, that for ten years past there has not been a cloud between me and my Saviour.'

Frances Ridley Havergal expressed her experience in verse:

> I never thought it could be thus,
> Month after month to know

> The river of Thy peace, without
> A ripple in its flow.

It may rightly be pointed out that these were special people but although that is true, their experience does set before us the possibility of attaining a fellowship with the Lord that is immeasurably closer than most of us are at present experiencing. God has no favourites.

Enthronement of Christ

Brief reference is made to Paul's statement in Romans 14:9, 'For this very reason, Christ died and returned to life so that *he might be the Lord* of both the dead and the living' (italics mine).

Could words express more simply and explicitly the ultimate purpose of the cross? In the previous passages under consideration, Christ's purpose *for us* has been in view. In this verse the focus is on the purpose of His death *for Himself*—sovereignty over the lives of those for whom He died. Even this purpose has an unselfish end in view, for true freedom can be enjoyed only in the life over which He is sovereign Lord.

Peter stated as an indisputable fact: 'He is Lord of all,' but He yearns for our spontaneous and practical recognition of that fact in daily life. Perhaps because of inadequate and defective teaching, the implications of discipleship have not been fully recognized and respected. We seem to have produced in the Church too many who desire all the benefits of Christ's Saviourhood, but are unwilling to bow to His sovereignty. Logically one cannot accept Christ as Saviour while rejecting Him as Lord.

Paul makes this crystal clear: 'If you confess with your mouth, 'Jesus is Lord,' and believe in your heart that God raised him from the dead, you will be saved (Rom 10:9). The day is assuredly coming when 'every knee shall bow and every tongue confess that Jesus Christ is Lord', but He longs that before that day there should be a voluntary coronation rather than a compulsory recognition.

Ideally, that coronation should accompany conversion, but if His claim to lordship over our life was not fully recognized at that time, then we should enthrone Him as Lord of our life as soon as His sovereign rights are recognized.

William Borden (the young American millionaire who died while preparing to engage in missionary work among the Muslims of China under the China Inland Mission) wrote these words in an act of coronation of His Lord which we may well emulate:

> Lord Jesus, I take hands off as far as my life is concerned. I put Thee on the throne of my heart. Change, cleanse me, use me as Thou shalt choose.[3]

When Jesus was on earth he claimed he would atone for our sin. In time the hour of his crucifixion came and Jesus died. The sacrifice was offered, the atonement made. But how were human beings to know it was acceptable? Suppose that Jesus himself had sinned, even while hanging on the cross. In that case the Lamb would not have been without spot or blemish, and the atonement would not have been perfect. Will God accept the sacrifice?

For three days the question remains unanswered. Then the moment of the resurrection comes. The hand of God reaches down into the cold Judean tomb, and the body of Christ is quickened. He rises. The stone is rolled away. Jesus is exalted to the right hand of the Father. By these acts we know that God has accepted the perfect sacrifice of his Son for sin.[1]

James M. Boice

7

The Purpose of Christ's Resurrection

He was raised on the third day (1 Cor 15:4).

On a Good Friday morning several decades ago, the residents of a district of London were confronted on their way to church with a question they found exhibited on walls, doors and fences: *'Will faith in a dead man save you?'*

The bills on which the question appeared were posted by adherents of a well-known secularist society. They were insinuating that since Christ had died on the cross, belief in Him and Christianity based on Him were an insult to commonsense.

But any intelligent Christian would have given the same answer to the question as those who asked it—a resounding 'no'! For Christianity's fundamental belief is enshrined in the Saviour's own words: 'I am the Living One; I was dead, and behold I am alive for ever and ever' (Rev 1:18). The Christian willingly concedes that if Christ is not risen from the dead, his faith is empty and futile, and he is of all men the most miserable.

For the Christian, Easter is the most significant week of the church year since it highlights the three great facts that constitute the basis of our faith. Each of these facts is on the same level of historical value. In his powerful apologetic on the resurrection, Paul states that 'Christ died for our sins according to the Scriptures, that he was buried, that he was raised on the third day according to the Scriptures' (1 Cor 15:3-4).

Outside the city wall of Jerusalem, Jesus of Nazareth died on the cross on the first Good Friday. On the Saturday He lay in Joseph's new tomb. On the first day of the new week He rose from the dead, having conquered death, Satan and Hades. If any one of these facts is not literally true, then, instead of being Good News, Christianity is a tissue of lies, based on chicanery and deceit. On the other hand, if it can be shown that Jesus actually rose from the dead, as the Scriptures claim, then Christianity rests on an impregnable foundation.

The historical basis

Christianity is an historical religion based on historical facts, and the Church of our day has no more urgent need than to recover belief in Christ's resurrection as an historical fact, and to proclaim it as fearlessly as did the apostles, who personally saw Him 'alive after His passion'.

In this connection, J. Russell Howden pointed out that there are three orders of facts, each admitting and requiring its own appropriate method of proof:[2]

1. *Mathematical facts,* for which the appropriate proof is pure reasoning.
2. *Scientific facts,* whose appropriate method of proof is by experiment.
3. *Historical facts,* for which there are four appropriate proofs:
   (a) The evidence of eye-witnesses
   (b) Institutions which had their rise in the alleged fact

(c) Customs with a similar origin
(d) Material remains

Historical facts are not subject to proof by experiment, so it would be illogical to demand scientific proof of the resurrection. When we adopt the appropriate method of proof, however, the resurrection emerges as a wholly credible happening, for it rests on good authority, reliable facts, and competent and disinterested eye-witnesses. The importance the apostles attached to that event, and the sincerity of their belief may be gauged by the prominence they accorded it in their teaching and preaching.

What do evangelical Christians mean by 'the resurrection of Christ'? Do they mean merely that His spirit survived death? Or that He spiritually manifested Himself to His disciples? No, indeed. That would not be a resurrection. Their belief is that 'Christ in the totality of His personality came back to them; that His spirit, leaving Hades, again took possession of His body, and raised it from the grave'.[3]

But there are many who deny the factuality of the bodily resurrection of Christ. It is not that they have found the evidence insufficient, but that *they have rejected the evidence on the assumed a priori grounds that such a resurrection is impossible.* Such an attitude is quite unscientific and unreasonable. Surely the scientific method is first to examine the facts, and then to form a theory in the light of them. The other approach is only an expression of the general disbelief in the supernatural.

This disbelief is not shared by a great many scholars of all the disciplines. The testimony of one such scholar, Sir Edward Clarke, a noted British jurist, presents another picture:

> As a lawyer I have made prolonged study of the evidence for the events of the first Easter Day. To me the evidence is conclusive, and over and over again in the High Court I have

secured the verdict on evidence not nearly so compelling. Inference follows on evidence, and a truthful witness is always artless and disdains effect. The Gospel evidence for the resurrection is of this class, and as a lawyer I accept it unreservedly as the testimony of truthful men to facts they were able to substantiate.[4]

The resurrection narratives themselves have the ring of truth about them. Although they are independent records, they are harmonious, and give the impression of being the reliable stories of eye-witnesses.

Physical or spiritual resurrection?

Some who would affirm that they believe in resurrection, maintain that Christ's was a spiritual, not a physical, resurrection. Others hold that whether Jesus lives in a body or only in spirit, is unimportant—the only thing that matters is that He is alive.

But is this really so? The theory that the post-resurrection body of Jesus was intangible and non-substantial and not a material body, is in direct conflict with our Lord's own categorical statement: 'A ghost does not have flesh and bones, as you see I have' (Lk 24:39). He was no ghost or phantom.

It is true that Paul said the body of the believer is 'raised a spiritual body' (1 Cor 15:44), but this is not synonymous with a spiritual resurrection. (In any case, is not 'a spiritual resurrection' a contradiction in terms? If the spirit cannot die, how can it be raised?) The Greek word for 'body' is used ten times in this chapter, and always in the sense of a material body. The only place in the New Testament where it bears a different meaning, is when it refers to the mystical body of Christ.

The disciples had no doubt of the reality and tangibility of His resurrection body. Mary had clung to Him. He had eaten and drunk with His men. He challenged them to touch His body and test its reality. These were indisputable proofs of a material, although transformed, body. It transcended normal physical limitations, for now the physical was under the control of the spiritual.

It was the same body, for nothing of the old body remained in the tomb. Its identity could be recognized by the tragic wounds. But it was different in that now it could materialize or immaterialize at will. While there was an essential continuity, there was yet a mysterious difference, the full explanation of which must await the life beyond.

> Coming the dead to seek, amazed, they found
>   Two shining angels witnessing with joy
> Their risen Lord. Their rapture knew no bound
>   Back to their brethren in His loved employ
> In haste they ran, the glorious news to spread,
> That Christ had risen from the dead.
>
> *Lewis H. Court*

Evidences of the resurrection

Of the many relevant lines of proof, the following are some of the more important ones. While any one of these may not be thought sufficient of itself to establish the certainty of the resurrection, taken together they constitute a demonstration of overwhelming force.

The testimony of Jesus

On a number of occasions, in conversation with His disciples, Jesus foretold His resurrection. At first the references were indirect, as in the cryptic statement: 'Destroy this temple, and I will raise it again in three days . . . but the temple he had spoken of was his body' (Jn 2:19,21).

Later He spoke more plainly, staking His credibility as a prophet on this improbable prediction:

> The Son of Man will be betrayed to the chief priests and the teachers of the law. They will condemn him to death and will

turn him over to the Gentiles to be mocked and flogged and crucified. On the third day he will be raised to life! (Mt 20:18-19).

To the cynical Jews who demanded a further sign in support of His Messianic claims, Jesus used Jonah's experience with the fish as a type of His burial and resurrection:

As Jonah was three days and three nights in the belly of a huge fish, so the Son of Man will be three days and three nights in the heart of the earth (Mt 12:40).

His enemies gave more credence to His prediction than did His disciples:

The chief priests and the Pharisees went to Pilate. 'Sir,' they said, 'we remember that while he was still alive that deceiver said, 'After three days I will rise again.' So give the order for the tomb to be made secure until the third day. Otherwise, his disciples may come and steal the body and tell the people that he has been raised from the dead. This last deception will be worse than the first.'

'Take a guard,' Pilate answered. 'Go, make the tomb as secure as you know how.' So they went and made the tomb secure by putting a seal on the stone and posting the guard (Mt 27:63-66).

But in spite of all their precaution, the tomb could not hold its prey.

> Vain the stone, the watch, the seal!
>   Hallelujah!
> Christ hath burst the gates of hell:
>   Hallelujah!
> Death in vain forbids Him rise;
>   Hallelujah!
> Christ hath opened Paradise—
>   Hallelujah!

The vacant tomb

The women who had come with Jesus from Galilee followed Joseph and saw the tomb and how his body was laid in it. . . .

On the first day of the week, very early in the morning, the women took the spices they had prepared and went to the tomb. They found the stone rolled away from the tomb, but when they entered, they did not find the body of the Lord Jesus (Lk 23:55; 24:1-3).

Such was the experience of the women.

What did Peter see when with characteristic impetuosity he burst into the tomb? In keeping with Jewish custom, the body of Jesus had been swathed in linen bandages which were impregnated with Joseph's one hundred pounds' weight of embalming spices. His head would be wrapped in a separate turban.

When Peter entered the tomb:

He saw the strips of linen lying there, as well as the burial cloth that had been around Jesus's head. The cloth was folded up by itself, separate from the linen (Jn 20:6-7).

What he saw was just like a chrysallis that had been abandoned by the butterfly.

One of the most interesting circumstantial proofs of the Resurrection [wrote Samuel M. Zwemer] is the curious statement in John's Gospel (20:7), 'and the napkin that was about his head, not lying with the linen clothes, but wrapped together (Greek, 'coiled round and round') in a place by itself'. No one can study the Greek and fail to see what is implied. The cloth had been folded around Jesus' head in burial as a turban is folded, and it lay by itself in that form when the other linen had been laid aside, just as when they go to sleep, Arabs and other Orientals put the turban off without disengaging its folds.[5]

How could the absence of the body be explained? The state in which the cloths were found, together with the fact that the tomb had been sealed and guarded, precluded the possibility of it having been stolen. The absent body and the collapsed grave clothes convinced the hitherto incredulous disciples. 'Finally the other disciple, who had reached the tomb first, also went inside. *He saw and believed*' (Jn

20:8, italics mine).

The post-resurrection appearances

At least ten of Christ's appearances to His disciples are recorded in the New Testament. He was seen by all sorts of people, singly and in groups, by night and day, on sea and land, in all kinds of places. On one occasion 'he appeared to more than five hundred of the brothers at the same time', and, Paul adds, 'most of whom are still living' (1 Cor 15:6). So he knew personally many of these witnesses to the resurrection. It is unreasonable to think that all these competent witnesses were mistaken.

The observance of the Lord's day

The strict observance of the Sabbath was of vast importance in Jewish worship. It was what they considered our Lord's loose attitude towards the Sabbath that evoked their deep hostility. A Jew would rather die than fight on the Sabbath. So how is such a revolutionary change as the substitution of the Christian Lord's Day for the sacred Jewish Sabbath explained? What cause was sufficiently influential to produce such a startling effect? The answer is simple—the resurrection of Jesus.

'What brought about this change?' asks Harry Rimmer.

> The answer is self-evident, historical, clear. Jesus Christ, by rising from the dead on the first day of the week, gave His Church a new event to commemorate. It may be well for the Jew to hold in memory the finished work of creation, but the Christian worships God Almighty because of the resurrection of Jesus Christ from the dead.[6]

The existence of the Christian Church

The fact of the Christian Church (which can today claim to be truly universal, for there is no nation of significance in which it is not established) has to be explained. This amazing phenomenon cannot just be brushed aside.

Its very existence is circumstantial evidence of a very convincing nature. How was it that within a few weeks of the death of a discredited religious leader who had been executed as a common criminal, there emerged a society closely-knit around His name in the very scene of their defeat? What caused the sudden transformation in those terrified men who had been utterly demoralized by His death, and had no expectation whatever of His resurrection? What caused them, in the face of bitter persecution and imminent torture and death, to continue preaching with overwhelming conviction that their Master had risen and was now alive?

What power changed Saul, the ruthless chief-persecutor of the Christians, into an ardent apostle of Christ overnight? Only irrefutable evidence would have satisfied the acute mind and overcome the bitter prejudice of a man who is considered one of the most brilliant intellects of all time.

The Church is the effect, what was the cause? In his book *Who Moved the Stone?* Frank Morison suggests an answer:

> Only from an intensely heated centre of burning zeal could this vast field of lava have been thrown out of a tiny country like Palestine, to the limits of the Roman world. We cannot insist on the strict rule of causality in the physical world, and deny it in the psychological.[7]

From the graves in the catacombs and other contemporary evidence, competent investigators have estimated that in the first three centuries A.D. at least twenty million had accepted the faith of a risen Lord. This Church arose out of belief in the resurrection, and the belief came out of the fact.

The purpose of the resurrection

The resurrection of Christ has relevance for us in relation to the past, the present and the future. Only as we discern its significance and purpose in these areas will we be able to exploit and experience all that God intends it should contribute to the life and service of His followers.

Concerning the past

It was a visible, historical demonstration of His deity, a convincing confirmation of His claim to be the Son of God. 'Through the Spirit of holiness [he] was declared with power to be the Son of God by his resurrection from the dead' (Rom 1:4). It was only after this event that the doubting Thomas confessed Christ's deity in the words: 'My Lord, and my God!'

Further, *it explained the meaning and efficacy of His death.* The resurrection was God's certification that Jesus had accomplished the mission on which He had been sent, and had finished it to the Father's complete satisfaction. He emerged from the tomb, not as an emaciated convalescent, but as complete Conqueror of death and Victor over Satan. Only by the resurrection of His body could it have been shown, without doubt, that death was utterly conquered, and a door opened to eternal life.

Concerning the present

The resurrection *revealed and released a new power for holy living.* Paul's prayer for his Ephesian friends was that they might come to know

> His incomparably great power for us who believe. That power is like the working of his mighty strength, which he exerted in Christ when he raised him from the dead (Eph 1:19-20).

Paul was prepared to make any sacrifice if only he might come 'to know Christ and the power of his resurrection' (Phil 3:10). And what a reservoir of power that event made available for him and for us!

It also affords the believer *the assurance of companion-*

ship on the pathway of life. Before He rose, Jesus had promised His disciples, 'I will not leave you as orphans; I will come to you' (Jn 14:18). After His resurrection, He renewed the assurance: 'Surely I will be with you always, to the very end of the age' (Mt 28:20). We can draw daily comfort and challenge from His living presence with us.

Concerning the future

His death and resurrection *banish the fear of death.* He rendered powerless him who held the power of death, that is the devil, and delivered 'those who all their lives were held in slavery by their fear of death' (Heb 2:15). Henceforth for the believer there is no death, in the full sense of that word, only 'sleep'. In place of craven fear of death, the resurrection imparts a living hope. 'He has given us new birth into a living hope through the resurrection of Jesus Christ from the dead' (1 Pet 1:3).

> The fear of death has gone for ever
> No more to make my soul to grieve,
> There is a place I do believe
> In heaven for me beyond the river
> My soul has found a resting place
> And I am now through heavenly grace
> At peace with God
>
> *R. Slater*

Through His death and resurrection Jesus not only abolished death, but He also *'brought life and immortality to light* through the gospel' (2 Tim 1:10, italics mine). Immortality means more than endless existence, for it is concerned with quality of life as well as quantity. It is not a mere endless extension of this life.

Finally, His resurrection is *the pledge that we too shall rise.* 'The one who raised the Lord Jesus from the dead will also raise us with Jesus and will bring us with you in his presence' (2 Cor 4:14).

Ian Maclaren tells of two pictures he saw in a Paris salon. One represented a king lying on his death-bed. He had just died, and his servants, who a moment before had trembled at his word, are now rifling his caskets and wardrobe. Beneath the pictures are the words: 'William the Conqueror.' What a conqueror! Just a moment dead and his own servants were despoiling him!

The other picture represented a Man lying in a rocky tomb, also dead; but angels were keeping watch, and to that tomb, now empty, all ages and generations come. He, the Christ, was the true Conqueror and His the glorious victory.[8]

> Christ Jesus lay in death's strong bands
>   For our offences given;
> But now at God's right hand He stands,
>   And brings us life from heaven
> Wherefore let us joyful be,
>   And sing to God right thankfully,
> Loud songs of Hallelujah!
>   *Martin Luther*

How natural, how easy, how artless His manifestations were through those blessed forty days! How quietly He dropped down among them, unheralded, unassuming, unattended by angelic guards and sometimes undistinguished from themselves, in His simple presence. . . . See Him on the way to Emmaus! How naturally He drops in on the little company as they walk. How unaffectedly He talks with them. How easily He turns the conversation to heavenly themes, and yet how free from strain His every word and attitude. All they were conscious of is a strange burning in their hearts and a kindling warmth of love.[1]

A.B. Simpson

8

The Purpose of Christ's Post-Resurrection Ministry

> After his suffering, he showed himself to these men and gave
> many convincing proofs that he was alive. He appeared to
> them over a period of forty days and spoke about the kingdom
> of God (Acts 1:3).

The period between our Lord's resurrection and ascension
to His Father's right hand, links two worlds. It marks the
transition between His earthly life and His heavenly ministry, and affords valuable insight into the mind and purpose
of God for His disciples.

There is much more revealed in Scripture concerning the
happenings of this brief but epochal period than super-
ficially appears, and their importance should not be under-
estimated. Compressed into these few crucial days were
experiences that prepared the disciples for the world-
embracing task that lay ahead.

Our Lord's conversations with His disciples in the inter-
val of the forty days was marked by simplicity and mystery.
His words seemed to convey the impression that they contained a deeper and hidden meaning, as indeed they did.

Even after the astounding miracle of the resurrection,

the disciples were hankering after a tangible Jewish monarchy with its trappings of pomp and power, rather than
anticipating their Master's triumphant ascension into
heaven. 'Lord, are you at this time going to restore the
kingdom to Israel?' was their earthly inquiry.

Their conception of Christ's kingdom was still in terms of
temporal power, and it took the upheaval of Pentecost to
spiritualize their conceptions and kindle new spiritual life.
So utterly had their preconceived Messianic expectations
collapsed, that even the angelic announcement of the
resurrection had failed to dispel their gloom. It took His
repeated appearances to accustom their thinking to the
new relationship that existed between them.

The question naturally arises: *did Jesus appear to His
disciples in His glorified body,* or did He assume that only
after His ascension?

It has been plausibly suggested that the Gospel records
afford no support for the theory of a change in our Lord's
resurrection body before His ascension. The implication is
that the reason for the disciples' failure to recognize Him
on some occasions, and Mary being unable to distinguish
Him from the gardener, lay in them rather than in Him.

From Christ's words we would conclude that the reason
for Cleopas and his companion failing to recognize Him on
the Emmaus road was a subjective one. It was not that He
had changed but that 'they were kept from recognizing
him'. Later, it is recorded, 'their eyes were opened and
they recognized him and he disappeared out of their sight'
(Lk 24:16,31). The fact that He ate and drank with them
would seem to support the view that the transformation
and glorification of the Lord's body took place when He
ascended into Heaven.

The purpose of the appearances

What fact or factor revolutionized the outlook and deter-

mined the future ministry of the dejected disciples? Was it
not the vision and repeated appearances of a risen Christ?
The main objective of His post-resurrection appearances
was to encourage and equip them for future ministry, and
to prepare them for the coming change in their relationship. When He said to Mary, 'Do not hold on to me, for I
have not yet returned to the Father' (Jn 20:17), He was
indicating that His leaving them was an occasion for joy,
not sorrow; for gain, not loss.

Observe some of our Lord's objectives in these repeated
appearances:

*1. To convince His still half-incredulous disciples that the
tomb was really empty,* and that they were not hallucinat-
ing. He presented to their senses unmistakable evidence of
His survival after death. He employed the familiar look,
gesture and tone of voice to convince them. He talked with
them, ate with them, walked with them in natural and
uninhibited fellowship.

He demonstrated His physical identity by displaying the
livid scars in hands and feet. Sight, touch and hearing
combined to place the fact of His resurrection beyond
reasonable doubt. His appearances thus held evidential
value in confirming the fact of the resurrection.

2. To display His universal authority. It was during the
forty days that He made the audacious claim: 'All authority
in heaven and on earth has been given to me' (Mt 28:18).
Every kind of power, celestial and terrestrial.

Paul pinpoints the time when Christ was invested with
this universal authority. 'He was declared with power to be
the Son of God by the resurrection from the dead.' Because
He possessed this authority He was able to delegate it to the
disciples He sent out. 'I have given you authority . . . to
overcome all the power of the enemy' (Lk 10:19). Their
witness could therefore be authoritative as well as
apologetic.

3. To assure them of His perpetual spiritual presence with them. It was during this period that Jesus gave His missionary commission with its accompanying assurance: 'Therefore go and make disciples of all nations . . . and surely I will be with you always, to the very end of the age' (Mt 28:19-20).

It should be noted that the fulfilment of that promise and obedience to the command are interdependent. It was only as they were engaged in making disciples of all nations that they could count on the strengthening presence of the Lord. The promise cannot be plucked from its context and claimed without qualification.

The Lord also made it clear to His followers that His future relation with them would be on a spiritual, not a physical, basis. His physical presence would be withdrawn, but He would be spiritually present with them through His Spirit. When Mary recognized Jesus and rapturously cried, 'Rabboni!' Jesus told her not to cling to Him, because he had not yet ascended to the Father, but to go to the brothers and prepare them for His ascension. She reluctantly discovered that henceforth hers would be a new relationship to Him.

4. *To reassure them of His unchanged attitude.* He was still 'this same Jesus', quite unchanged in His loving concern for His own. This fact was demonstrated in His gentleness with Mary, His loving faithfulness with penitent Peter, His thoughtful concern when He cooked the breakfast for the famished fishermen. Death had not changed His attitude or altered His disposition. His tender, solicitous love had survived the grave.

But though they recognized in Him the same loving Friend, they displayed a greater awe and reverence in His presence. 'None of the disciples ventured to question him, "Who are you?" knowing that it was the Lord.' When Mary recognized Him, she simply gasped, 'Master!' Thomas later blurted out, 'My Lord and my God!'

5. *To clarify their conception of the spiritual nature of the*

kingdom of God. During the forty days, His great pre-occupation was speaking of the concerns of the kingdom of God. In doing this, He did not concentrate on methods of work, or publicity, or fund-raising campaigns, or organizational programmes. He focused their attention on the great principles and essentials which must be their concern if His Father's purpose for the world was to be realized. The coming of the kingdom must be their preoccupation as well as His.

6. *To excite them with His missionary programme.* The happenings and conversations that took place during this period afforded clear evidence that death had not caused His missionary concern to abate. It survived and was perpetuated by the resurrection. His deep passion and concern for men whom He saw as lost, was to find continuing expression through the ministry of His yet-incredulous disciples.

This global missionary concern is compressed into a few pregnant commands that carry the full weight of His divine authority. Here they are, one from each of the Gospels.

'Go and make disciples of all nations.'

'Go into all the world and preach the good news to all creation.'

'Repentance and forgiveness of sins will be preached in his name to all the nations.'

'As the Father has sent me, I am sending you.'

Evidence of the harmony and interdependence of the members of the Godhead in working out man's redemption, is seen in the fact that, even after the resurrection, the Lord gave these commandments to His followers 'through the Holy Spirit' (Acts 1:2).

The all-inclusiveness of His programme staggers the imagination: all the nations—all the world—all creation. Into the hands of His weak but devoted disciples, the Lord entrusted the stupendous task of world-evangelization. How greatly they would need His supporting presence and dynamic power if this ambitious programme were ever to be realized.

He clearly stated the nature and extent of their mission: 'You will be my witnesses in Jerusalem, and in all Judea and Samaria, and to the ends of the earth' (Acts 1:8). Their witness was to radiate from Jerusalem as a centre, in ever-widening circles, until it reached earth's remotest bound. So far as possible, their witness was to be synchronous in the regions mentioned.

The post-resurrection interviews

What were 'the concerns of the kingdom of God' that Jesus shared with His friends? What were the orders He gave to the apostles by the Holy Spirit (Acts 1:2-3)? Although the records are very condensed, a close look at what transpired during some of our Lord's appearances will shed some light on the subject.

When He appeared *to the seven* on the Sea of Tiberias (Jn 21:1), He granted them a remarkable and symbolic catch of fish, a catch so great that they were not able to haul it in. Earlier He had promised that if they followed Him, He would make them fishers of men. Now He teaches them through this incident that only as their service was Christ-directed, would they be successful in 'taking men alive'.

On appearing *to the ten* in the Upper Room in Jerusalem (Thomas was absent), His first act was to banish their fears and bestow His peace. He then made a startling announcement: 'As the father has sent me, I am sending you' (Jn 20:19-20). In a symbolic act He intimated that the Holy Spirit would be given as the source of their power.

> That night the apostles met in fear,
> Amidst them came their Lord most dear,
> And greeted them with words of cheer,
>   Hallelujah!
>
> *Jean Tisseraud*

To the eleven in Jerusalem, after saying that it was written: 'Repentance and forgiveness of sins will be preached in [Christ's] name to all nations, beginning at Jerusalem' (Lk 24:47), the risen Lord ordered them to await in the city the promised enduement of power, apart from which His plan for world-evangelization would inevitably founder.

Then Jesus appeared to *'more than five hundred of the brothers* at the same time' (1 Cor 15:6, italics mine), on a mountain in Galilee, and it was with this favoured group that He shared His ambitions and seemingly impossible programme.

His unqualified command, 'go out and make disciples of all nations', was and is both universal and individual, and is applicable to every believer. It was a call to strenuous and sacrificial endeavour. Missionary work cannot be done by proxy, and the sacrifices involved should be shared equally by those in the sending lands if the concerns of the kingdom are to be adequately cared for.

An analysis of the teaching Christ gave during the forty days reveals the following factors:
—He expected from His messengers unrivalled love, utter loyalty and unqualified obedience.
—He expected them to go personally to make disciples of all nations, or to stand loyally behind those who had gone.
—He undertook to supply the necessary dynamic.
—He promised them His perpetual presence while executing His commission.
—His emphasis was more on devotion to Himself than on devotion to the work or the programme.

Christ's self-revelation during the forty days

Many precious gems of truth arise incidentally out of the events of this significant period. Some of the more important are:
1. He is alive. 'After his suffering, he showed himself to

these men' (Acts 1:3). The Muslim proudly boasts to the Christian, 'We have what you do not have—the coffin of Muhammad, the founder of our religion, with his remains in Mecca.' This may be true, but the glory of Christianity is not in a full coffin, but in an empty tomb. Neither coffin nor tomb could permanently hold the Son of God.

2. *He is Conqueror* of death and Hades (Rev 1:18). With the weapon of His own death. He met and engaged in mortal combat with the massed forces of evil and emerged victorious. He broke for ever their grip on the human race, and now carries at His girdle the keys of death and Hades.

The reality of His conquest was seen in His effortless emergence from the strictly-guarded and securely-sealed rock tomb—without moving the stone. When He appeared time and again to His disciples, it was not as a haggard victim, as one would have expected under the circumstances, but as a radiant Conqueror with power to enthuse and inspire His despondent followers.

3. *Though divine, He is still human;* so human that Mary mistook Him for the gardener. Recognition awakened only when He called her name in those well-loved tones. During the forty days, His relations with His followers remained easy and relaxed. His conversation with the two on the Emmaus road was so ordinary and natural that they failed to recognize in the stranger their Lord and Master. What a human touch it was when he cooked the breakfast!

4. *He is all-powerful.* Behind His quiet, serene, restrained personality, there resides infinite authority and power. The forces of nature obey His words. Hell trembles at His name. Whatever authority the rulers of the world exercise is derived from His sovereign will, for 'he fixed the epochs of their history and the limits of their territory' (Acts 17:27, New English Bible).

5. *His love is eternal,* and therefore we need have no fear that He may abuse His absolute and sovereign power.

Note how tenderly He spoke to Mary: 'Woman, why are

you crying?' How thoughtful of Him to seek out the heart-broken Peter and grant him a personal counselling session that healed his hurt. How patient and lovingly perceptive He was with disbelieving Thomas as He held out His hands for inspection. This indeed is love that passes knowledge.

> Mine is an unchanging love,
> Higher than the heights above,
> Deeper than the depths beneath,
> Sure and steadfast, strong as death.
> *William Cowper*

6. *He is perpetually present,* and will be so 'even to the end of the age'. We are not moving on merely to the *termination* of the age but to its *consummation.* The age could be terminated with little having been achieved. But it will find its consummation in the fulfilment of the eternal purpose of God—the coronation of His Son and the estab-lishment of His kingdom.

> One Lord, one empire, all secures;
> He reigns, and death and life are yours;
> Through earth and heaven one song shall ring,
>   'The Lord omnipotent is King!'
> *Josiah Conder*

Christ's disciples did not see Him rise from the dead, but they did see Him ascend into heaven. For the confirmation of the certainty and reality of the resurrection, it was not necessary that they should see Him rise, but only that they should see Him risen. But it *was* necessary that they should see Him ascend in order to be sure that He had ascended. In the one case they saw the effect, but not the act; and in the other case they saw the act, but not the effect.

All we are told is that Jesus left His disciples as He had never left them before. Up or down, indicating direction, will not bear scientific scrutiny, but that which matters is plain, that He who came into the world went from it, and never since has been physically in it. [1]

W. Graham Scroggie

9
The Purpose of Christ's Ascension

> When he ascended on high, he led captives in his train and gave gifts to men (Eph 4:8).

Although it is specifically mentioned only three times in the Gospels, the ascension of our Lord was a tremendously important event in His life and ministry. It was of great significance in the scheme of redemption, and is consequently important to the Christian. Apart from these specific references, there are, however, eleven other allusions to it in the New Testament.

The ascension of Christ is defined as that event in which the risen Christ visibly withdrew from His disciples and passed into the heavens at the close of His ministry on earth. It marked His entry into the divine glory and, together with the crucifixion and the resurrection, was part of God's great redemptive act.

Like some other facts of Scripture, no attempt is made to prove it. It is asserted and assumed as a real historical event, a fact of Christ's life as real as any other. While it appears less dramatic than the resurrection, it is its necessary complement.

117

> We feel and grasp its fitness, its necessity, as the one possible
> sequel to the Resurrection [wrote H.C.G. Moule]. We handle
> the firm texture of contemporary truth in the narrative, in
> which the extreme economy of attendant wonders is a sure sign
> of the absence of mythical alloy.

The ascension may also be said to be complementary to
the incarnation through which the union of God and man
was effected. In the words of Rabbi Duncan, the dust of
earth is on the throne of the Majesty on high.

Our Lord's assumption into heaven was the appropriate
climax to the kind of life He lived, and to such a death as He
died. He could claim that He had left no promise of God
dishonoured, no prophecy unfulfilled, and no demand un-
met. The method of His departure was in keeping with the
supernatural elements and miraculous achievements of His
life. It could probably be said that His departure into
heaven had more in common with the prolonged walk of
Enoch than with the departure of Elijah to the accompaniment of whirlwind and chariot of fire.

It is of interest that no fewer than thirteen different
words are employed to describe the mode of His ascension,
for example: 'taken up', 'received up', 'lifted up', 'borne'.
He had departed permanently and would have no immedi-
ate contact with the earth until His second advent.

The manner of the ascension

'He was taken up before their very eyes, and a cloud hid
him from their sight.' There could be no questioning the
reality of the event—it took place in broad daylight.
Bethany, the place where He enjoyed the most precious
earthly fellowship, was the scene of the final farewell.

It was important that His final departure should be different from His other disappearances during the forty days
—something more than just vanishing out of their sight—
otherwise there might linger in their minds the nagging

possibility the He might appear once again. There had to be a finality about it that would preclude such expectation. The purpose of His sporadic appearances and disappearances had been to accustom them to the reluctant prospect of His permanent departure.

In his commentary, J.P. Lange writes:

> The entrance and exit of Jesus Christ into and out of history could not be anything else than miraculous. His birth was not according to nature. His rising from the grave was contrary to the laws of nature. His ascension likewise transcended the laws of gravitation to which we are subject. But He is the Lord of creation!

From the meagre records we have, it appears that He began to walk away from His friends. Then He left them, and some manuscripts add: 'And was taken up into heaven.' They saw Him ascend before their very eyes. A cloud—Chrysostom called it the royal chariot—received Him out of their sight.

J.G. Davies wrote:

> The cloud into which Jesus is received is not a cloud of our atmosphere at all, but the vehicle of the divine presence, and Luke was thus affirming by the use of this imagery, that the Ascension was no more or less than the entry of Christ into the divine glory.[2]

It will be remembered that at the transfiguration 'a cloud appeared and enveloped them. . . . A voice came from the cloud . . .' (Lk 9:34-35). In that case, as well as in this, the cloud was in all likelihood the Shekinah which afforded the Israelites visible evidence of the presence of God in their desert travels. They now saw Jesus enveloped in the cloud of the divine glory.

> Lo! the heaven its Lord receives
> Yet He loves the earth He leaves;
> Though returning to His throne,
> Still He calls mankind His own. Alleluia!
>
> *Charles Wesley*

He ascended bodily, carrying into heaven His human, though now glorified, body. But though His body vanished from the sight of His disciples, His personal presence was mediated by the Holy Spirit. True, they had lost his *physical* presence, but in the coming of the Holy Spirit they would gain something better—His *spiritual* omni-presence. Had He not said in that very connection, 'I will not leave you as orphans: I will come to you'? Had He not assured His incredulous disciples, 'It is for your good that I am going away. Unless I go away, the Counsellor will not come to you' (Jn 14:18; 16:7)? Paradoxically, but actually, our Lord's presence in heaven means that He is more effectually present with His people on earth!

It is a comforting reflection that He ascended into heaven with hands outstretched, in the very act of blessing His own people, just as did the high priest under the Old Covenant. 'While he was blessing them, he left them and was taken up into heaven' (Lk 24:51). The moment His feet left the ground, He embarked on His continuing ministry of intercession.

> While He raised His hands in blessing,
>   He was parted from His friends;
> While their eager eyes beheld Him,
>   He upon the cloud ascends;
> He who walked with God and pleased him,
>   Preaching truth and doom to come,
> He, our Enoch, is translated
>   To His everlasting home.
>   *Christopher Wordsworth*

The necessity for the ascension

In the view of St Augustine, the festival of the ascension

> is that festival which confirms the grace of all festivals together, without which the profitableness of every festival would have purchased. For unless the Saviour had ascended into heaven.

His nativity would have come to nothing . . . and His passion would have borne no fruit for us, and His most holy resurrection would have been useless.[3]

There are many reasons why the ascension was necessary.

1. To fulfil the prophecies of the Old and New Testaments and the Lord's own predictions. Speaking by the inspiration of the Spirit, David had said, 'When you ascended on high, you led captives in your train' (Ps 68:18), and Paul associates this prediction with Christ in Ephesians 4:8. Jesus Himself predicted the event when He said, 'I am returning to my Father and your Father, to my God and your God' (Jn 20:17).

2. To complete the work of redemption. The four pillars on which the whole structure of Christianity rest are: the incarnation, the crucifixion, the resurrection and the ascension of Christ. Without the ascension, redemption would have been incomplete. How else could it be known that God's righteous claims against sinning men had been met and satisfied? Only in some such manner as this could the desperate problem created by man's sin find its final solution. How else could Christ be constituted the Head of the Church?

3. Such a denouement was necessary, for His unique and sinless personality demanded a departure from the world as appropriate as its entrance. To both Enoch and Elijah, a mysterious departure from earth was granted. How much more should this be the privilege of the Son of Man.

4. Because of the nature of His resurrection body. He could not depart from earth by way of physical dissolution, as do the rest of men. Such a body as His could not be permanently at home on earth for His departure involved the element of glorification.

5. Because only thus could His disciples give a plausible explanation of the disappearance of His body from the tomb. Speculation and theories were rampant, but the fact of His visible ascension was the strongest proof that He had really risen, and to this they could bear indisputable witness. His earthly ministry must be brought to an appropriate conclusion.

6. *To make possible the coming of the Holy Spirit.* Jesus indicated that the ascension was the essential condition of this blessing when He cried at the Feast of Tabernacles:

> 'Whoever believes in me, as the Scripture has said, streams of living water will flow from within him.' By this he meant the Spirit, whom those who believed in him were later to receive. Up to that time the Spirit had not been given, since Jesus had not yet been glorified (Jn 7:38-39).

Only after Jesus had ascended was the Spirit outpoured. Peter describes this influential event:

> Exalted to the right hand of God, he has received from the Father the promised Holy Spirit and has poured out what you now see and hear (Acts 2:33).

This was His crowning work in the whole plan of redemption.

7. *To bestow gifts on His Church.* 'When he ascended on high . . . [he] gave gifts to men' (Eph 4:8). Included in the gift of the Holy Spirit, were men supernaturally equipped by Him to minister to and build up the Church—apostles, prophets, evangelists, pastors and teachers. Through the Spirit, Christ also sovereignly bestowed on His followers a diversity of spiritual gifts to suit the multiplicity of their needs in discharging their office (1 Cor 12:11).

8. *That Jesus of Nazareth might be constituted the universal Head of the Church.*

> He raised him from the dead and seated him at his right hand in the heavenly realms . . . and appointed him to be head over everything for the church (Eph 1:20-22).

The purpose of the ascension

We self-centred mortals are apt to think more of what the great redemptive acts and facts of our faith mean to us than what they mean to the Lord Himself. To Him the ascension must have held great significance.

1. It was to Him the divine confirmation of His claim to full deity, a claim that had been challenged by man and devil. He had spoken of His impending ascension into heaven as His own prerogative, which He had temporarily renounced in the incarnation. Now He was free to reassert that prerogative, and His assumption into heaven was the seal of divine approval.

2. It was the divine compensation for His utter obedience to His father, and for His voluntary and vicarious death.

> He humbled himself and became obedient to death—even death on a cross! *Therefore* God exalted him to the highest place and gave him the name that is above every name (Phil 2:8-9).

His elevation was heaven's reversal of man's judgement on earth.

3. It was the divine credential that His mediatorial work was complete. The ascension was the evidence that He had done it to the Father's entire satisfaction. He returned to heaven as a Conqueror, leading in His train His vanquished captives. Now he is seated at God's right hand, not in indolent repose, but exercising the sovereign power and universal dominion He had won by the cross.

His ascension also had great significance for His followers then and now.

4. It afforded the disciples unassailable evidence that He carried our humanity back with Him into heaven. He assured them that though now physically removed from them, He would be spiritually near. His exaltation was the guarantee that all who are united to Him by faith will share His enthronement: 'Before long, the world will not see me live' (Jn 14:19).

5. *It gives assurance that He has defeated Satan and the powers of darkness,* for 'he led captive a host of captives'. He rescued those whom Satan held captive. The tyranny of sin had been shattered and its slaves liberated.

6. *It defined the nature of Christ's kingship.* His followers found it difficult to accept the fact that His kingship was not to be a temporal monarchy based on a ruthless use of power. Even the resurrection failed to purge them of their materialistic expectation of a powerful earthly king like David, who would shake off the yoke of Rome, and restore the kingdom to Israel. They were loath to embrace the idea of the Messiah being a suffering Servant. The ascension was designed to remove this misconception.

7. *It brought a sense of peace and assurance to His apprehensive disciples.* Hear Paul's bracing words:

> Who is he that condemns? Christ Jesus, who died—more than that, who was raised to life—is at the right hand of God and is also interceding for us (Rom 8:34).

8. *It made possible a more extensive work through His apostles than He Himself had achieved when on earth.* He had been limited by His human body, but He made the staggering prediction that must have mystified His disciples:

> I tell you the truth, anyone who has faith in me will do what I have been doing. He will do even greater things than these, because I am going to the Father (Jn 14:12).

Note that He did not say 'more spectacular miracles', but 'greater things'—moral and spiritual rather than miraculous. Not greater in spiritual quality, but more extensive and greater in quantity. And are not the works done in the souls of men the greatest? It has been said with justification that the spiritual conquests of the Church in succeeding ages, despite its weakness and failure, are a much greater display of divine power than even the miracles Jesus performed on earth. And all this has happened because He went to the Father.

9. It provided grounds for a sure hope for the future. How many generations of Christians have pillowed their heads on His promise:

> I am going there to prepare a place for you. And if I go and prepare a place for you, I will come back and take you to be with me that you also may be where I am (Jn 14:3).

10. It made available to His followers an inexhaustible supply of power and authority. He promised:

> 'You will receive power when the Holy Spirit comes on you; and you will be my witnesses . . . to the ends of the earth.' After he said this, *he was taken up before their very eyes,* and a cloud hid him from their sight (Acts 1:8, italics mine).

It is the marrow of our faith to remember that Jesus perfectly understands the nature of those whom He represents before God. To fully grasp this truth is to have open to us a well of comfort which is unfailing. To tell me that at the centre of the universe is One who bears my burdens and carries my sorrows; who knows the height and length and depth and breadth of human experience and need; who came into the world to teach me that compassion was the ruling characteristic of God; who knows my name, my weakness, my temperament, my surroundings; who is invested with universal authority that He may exercise on my behalf the succour and strength I need, is to tell me something that is good news indeed.[1]

J. Gregory Mantle

IO

The Purpose of Christ's Exaltation

Exalted to the right hand of God . . . (Acts 2:33).

Christ's ascension was the necessary preparatory step to His exaltation and glorification. It introduced Him into His present glorified state and mediatorial office.

The disproportionate space devoted in the Gospels to the death of Christ is clearest evidence of the vast importance *His finished work* holds in Christian faith and experience. But this costly work would have failed in its purpose apart from His presence in heaven to continue on our behalf *His unfinished work.* He died once for all, but He always lives to make intercession for us (Heb 7:25). His exaltation gives effect to the purpose for which He died.

God has raised this Jesus to life . . . *Exalted to the right hand of God,* he has received from the Father the promised Holy Spirit and has poured out what you now see and hear. For David did not ascend to heaven, and yet he said, 'The Lord said to my Lord: *'Sit at my right hand* until I make your enemies a footstool for your feet' (Acts 2:32-35, italics mine).

His mediatorial qualifications

From history's dawn, men have displayed an unsatisfied religious craving. They have been afflicted with a malaise that yearns for someone to act as priest or mediator between them and the god or gods whom they somehow feel they have offended, and who must be appeased. This despairing craving found poignant expression in the cry of the patriarch Job: 'If only there were someone to arbitrate between us, to lay his hand upon us both' (Job 9:33).

The logical outcome of this unsatisfied aspiration, was the creation of orders of priests, whom they hoped would be able to mediate for them. This concept reached its zenith in the Levitical order of priests at their best. But the tragic degeneration and prostitution of that sacred office resulted only in disillusionment. They came at last to realize that they must look elsewhere for the satisfaction of their secret yearning. The perfect answer to their instinctive desires was found only in Jesus.

It was the aim of the writer of the letter to the Hebrews to show that Christ alone was qualified to fill the role of great High Priest. He affirms that He holds this exalted office *by divine appointment*.

> No-one takes this honour upon himself; he must be called of God, just as Aaron was. So Christ also did not take upon himself the glory of becoming a high priest. But God who said to him, 'You are my son . . .' (Heb 5:4-5).

He was further qualified by reason of *His genuine identification with man* through His incarnation:

> Every high priest is selected from among men and is appointed to represent them in matters related to God . . . He is able to deal gently with those who are ignorant and are going astray, since he himself is subject to weakness (Heb 5:1-2).

Because He is linked with us in a common humanity, Christ is able to compassionately represent the human race before

God.

Further testimony to our Lord's competence to discharge this delicate ministry can be adduced: 'Such a high priest meets our need—one who is holy [worthily discharging His responsibility to God] blameless, pure, set apart from sinners, exalted above the heavens'—to the right hand of God (Heb 7:26).

His triumphant shout from the cross, 'Finished!' constituted the basis for His unfinished work of mediation and intercession. As our great High Priest, He was able to enter the Holiest of all with His own blood accompanied by the fragrant incense of a life of total devotion to God. Here is *the climax of the incarnation*—Jesus, the God-man, still clothed in the robes of our humanity, representing us before the eternal Father, and accepted by Him.

> He sits at God's right hand
>   Till all His foes submit,
> And bow to His command,
>   And fall beneath His feet
> We soon shall hear the archangel's voice;
> The trump of God shall sound; rejoice!
>
> *Charles Wesley*

Our need of His mediation

In his book, *The Lord's Anointed,* Henry de Vries writes:

There is an impression among some believers that our Lord's intercession is required only when we are in extreme need and danger, as Peter was when Satan desired to sift him as wheat, for then it was that Jesus prayed for him that his faith should not fail.

And this would be correct if our Lord's intercession were like the city fire department which is called on for help when the house is on fire. The fact is that our house is always on fire, and we are therefore always in need of intercession. There is not a moment when we are not in need and danger, and therefore our Lord lives for evermore to make intercession for us. His intercession never ceases and is always prevailing.[2]

What confidence it kindles in our hearts to know that at this very moment our heavenly Intercessor, who knows our frailty and enters into our feelings, is appearing for us in the presence of God.

The manner of His mediation

It is not uncommon for the idea of mediation and intercession to be associated with tearful entreaty, or with the erroneous concept of overcoming a supposed reluctance on the part of God. But Christ does not appear as a suppliant before a God who needs to be coaxed into compliance. He does not appear as our Advocate to plead for mercy, but to secure for us the justice which His sacrifice has won for us.

His intercession is not to be conceived as a *vocal* saying of prayers. Rather is it of the nature foreshadowed in the Levitical ritual of the great annual act of intercession on the Day of Atonement, during which the priest uttered not a word. The silence of the sanctuary was disturbed only by the tinkling bells on his vestment. It was not Aaron who was vocal, but the sacrificial blood that he sprinkled on the mercy seat. Even so is it the very presence of our great High Priest before the Father, still bearing in His glorified body the tangible evidence of His finished work, that speaks on our behalf. Charles Wesley puts it into these noble words:

> Five bleeding wounds He bears,
> Received on Calvary,
> They pour effectual prayers,
> They strongly plead for me.
> Forgive him! O forgive! they cry,
> Nor let the ransomed sinner die.

Our Lord intercedes for us *personally*. He delegates it to neither saints nor angels. The cares of the universe are not allowed to hinder Him attending to our petty concerns. As He was on earth, so He is in heaven. 'I am among you as one who serves' (Lk 22:27). It is He Himself who is our Mediator.

His intercession is *without intermission*. 'He always lives to intercede for them' (Heb 7:25). He lives to ensure that we receive the full benefits He secured for us by His cross. He does not give us His salvation as something separate from Himself.

His competence as intercessor

The deepest significance in the idea of priesthood lies in the ability of the priest to deal with sin and the problems it creates. The competence of Christ in this regard is wonderfully unfolded in the letter to the Hebrews.

He is competent to help those who are tempted.

And who of us is immune from temptation? Who does not need someone to aid in the lonely hour when temptation strikes or tribulation engulfs? Christ is that someone 'because he himself suffered when he was tempted, he is able to help those who are being tempted' (Heb 2:18).

There are two Greek verbs used to express Christ's intercession. The first, *parakaleo,* means 'to call to one's side'. The word is used of our Lord in 1 John 2:1: 'We have one who speaks to the Father in our defence—Jesus Christ, the Righteous One.' In this sense, the paraclete is one who comes in answer to a call of need.

The second word is *eutuchanein,* and carries the meaning 'to present oneself unsought'. The act of the Good Samaritan would be a good illustration of the latter word. It is also used in Romans 8:27: 'The Spirit intercedes for the saints in accordance with God's will.' Taken together, these words assure us that as our Mediator and Intercessor, Christ often comes to our aid unasked, as well as in response to our cry of need. Was this not what He did when He prayed for Peter—that his faith might not fail—even before he was called on to face the test?

We are often more than willing to help those in need of aid, but we are not always able. Our High Priest knows no such limitations. It should be noticed that His ability to help is not based on mere pity, but on costly propitiation. It was for this reason that

> He had to be made like his brothers in every way, in order that he might . . . make atonement for the sins of the people. [Therefore] he is able to help those who are tempted (Heb 2:17-18).

He is competent to have compassion on us in our weakness.

> For we do not have a high priest who is unable to sympathise with our weaknesses, but we have one who has been tempted in every way, just as we are—yet was without sin (Heb 4:15).

Our Lord's deity secures for us His never-ceasing presence and power, while His humanity assures us of His *compassion* and *sympathy*. These words, one from the Latin and the other from the Greek, mean much more than 'to be sorry for' another. They embody the thought of entering into the experience of the other person as though it were one's own.

This concept of God knows no parallel in Greek and pagan thought. They conceived of their gods as having a complete inability to feel and share their woes. They thought that the essential nature of their gods placed them beyond all feeling, and that they were completely detached and unaffected by the sufferings of mankind.

What a different picture this passage from Hebrews presents—a God who not only knows how we feel, but who actually shares that feeling with us—sin always excepted. We must note that it is with our *weaknesses* and infirmities that He sympathizes, *never with our sins*. Sin is not an essential part of human nature, but an intruder, for Jesus was truly human, yet was without sin. He understands the moral and physical weaknesses of our human constitution that make us so easily susceptible to sin; that sap our resistance and make it easy to succumb; for our weaknesses, if unduly pandered to, very easily degenerate into actual sin.

> Our fellow-sufferer yet retains
> A fellow-feeling for our pains,
> And still remembers in the skies
> His tears, His agonies and cries.
>
> In every pang that rends the heart
> The Man of Sorrows has a part;
> He sympathizes with our grief.
> And to the sufferer sends relief.
>
> *Scottish paraphrase*

The very fact that Jesus was tempted in all points as we are, brings Him very close to us—and us very close to Him. Like ourselves He felt the tremendous pressure of temptation, but unlike Him we all too often yield to its seductions. He too had to trust his Father in the dark, as when He uttered that desolated question, 'Why didst Thou forsake Me?' He too had to face the grim hour of death—and such a death!

So, in the compassion of our great Mediator and Intercessor, there coalesces the infinite love of God and the tenderness of a fellow-sufferer.

He is competent to save us completely and for ever

> Because Jesus lives for ever, he has a permanent priesthood. Therefore he is able to save completely those who come to God through him, *because he always lives to intercede for them* (Heb 7:24-25, italics mine).

The words translated 'completely' occur elsewhere only in Luke 13:11: 'A woman was there who . . . was bent over and could not straighten up *at all*.' G.H. Lang suggests the meaning to be that she could not 'completely' lift herself up. She was not so crippled as to be on her back all the time, yet she could move about only bowed down.[3] This is a condition reflected spiritually in too many Christians to-day—the face downward, minding earthly things, and powerless to 'completely' lift themselves up to God. But Christ is able to save us *completely,* a salvation that includes body, soul and spirit in its wide sweep.

Our great Intercessor is *both willing and able* to save us from sins of thought and feeling as well as of action. He is able to deal with the troublesome subconscious as well as the conscious. He can save from long-standing evil habits that have laughed at our new resolutions time and again.

Further, He is able to keep on saving us, for that is the force of the tense of the verb. The reason is that there is never a moment when His High-Priestly activities are in abeyance. Under the Old Covenant the priesthood was disrupted by death and sin, but Christ's New Covenant priesthood is uninterrupted and changeless. It is not trans-missible to another, nor can it be delegated to any human being.

He is competent as our High Priest and Mediator

He receives our prayers and praises, and presents them to His Father.

> Another angel, who had a golden censer, came and stood at the altar. He was given much incense to offer, with the prayers of all the saints, on the golden altar before the throne. The smoke of the incense, together with the prayers of the saints, went up before God from the angel's hand (Rev 8:3-4).

Because only the High Priest could minister at the golden altar of incense, it has been thought that 'the angel' was none other than Christ Himself, who accepts our Spirit-prompted prayers as His own, adds to them the virtue of His own merits, and presents them before the throne.

> To all our prayers and praises,
>   Christ adds His sweet perfume,
> And love the altar raises,
>   These odours to consume.

His High-Priestly blessing

There was another function of the Aaronic priesthood that carried over into our Lord's heavenly ministry. It was the function of the High Priest to *bless the people*. The blessing he pronounced was what is known as the Aaronic Benediction:

> The Lord bless you and keep you;
> The Lord make his face shine upon you
>   and be gracious to you;
> The Lord turn his face towards you
>   And give you peace (Num 6:24-26).

The corresponding New Covenant blessing is contained in the Apostolic Benediction: 'May the grace of the Lord Jesus Christ, and the love of God, and the fellowship of the Holy Spirit be with you all' (2 Cor 13:14).

From His position of celestial power and authority, Christ makes that blessing actual to His Church on earth. The disciples' last view of Him, ascending into heaven with hands outstretched, was typical of the ministry on which He had now entered—indicating blessing to those whom He had redeemed. By His cross He removed the curse. In His intercession He bestows the blessing.

It is of more than passing significance that in the Aaronic Benediction the High Priest's pronouncement of the blessing is followed up and ratified by Jehovah Himself in the words, 'And I will bless him' (v.27). But we must never forget the reason for which God bestowed this blessing on His people: 'I will bless you . . .*and you will be a blessing*' (Gen 12:2, italics mine).

How then should we understand what happened on Pentecost morning? We should not see the essence of this epoch-making event in the tornado sound, the sight of tongues of fire over each person's head, and the gift of language (these were secondary matters, what we might call the trimmings). We should see the essence of it, rather, in the fact that at nine o'clock in the morning the Holy Spirit's new covenant ministry began, giving each disciple a clear understanding of Jesus' place in God's plan, a robust sense of identity and authority as Jesus' person in this world, and an unlimited boldness in proclaiming Jesus' power from His throne—the new elements that are so amazing in Peter's sermon when we recall what sort of man he had been before.

Jesus had promised that when the Spirit came, He would empower the disciples for witness (Acts 1:5,8); and Luke evidently means us to see in Peter, whose failures he had diligently chronicled in his gospel, a model instance of that power being fulfilled.[1]

J.I. Packer

I I

The Purpose of Pentecost

When the day of Pentecost came . . . all of them were filled
with the Holy Spirit (Acts 2:1,4).

Far from bringing down the curtain on the ministry of
Jesus, His ascension and exaltation merely introduced
another and more exciting phase of it. In his Gospel, Luke
recounts what Jesus *began* to do and teach. In his second
book, the Acts of the Apostles, he records what He *continued* to do and teach through the agency of the Holy Spirit
and His mystical Body, the Church.

In my former book, Theophilus, I wrote about all that Jesus
began to do and to teach until the day he was taken up to
heaven, after giving instructions *through the Holy Spirit* to the
apostles he had chosen (Acts 1:1-2, italics mine).

We are therefore justified in saying that the day of Pentecost, with its attendant events, was but a continuation, an
extension of our Lord's ministry, for Pentecost was the
necessary complement of Calvary. It constituted an essential stage in accomplishing the global purpose of the risen
and ascended Lord.

A study of the history of the Church reveals that every significant advance in power and service has begun with a return to the message, and a recovery of the power that characterized the founders of the Church. The dynamic released at Pentecost is still available to all who are prepared to obey the laws of spiritual power, and such a rediscovery could be the precursor of revival in our day.

Michael Green envisages such a possibility:

> Just as there was a great outpouring of the Spirit at the coming of the Messiah, so at the beginning of the age of the Church's witness-bearing to Jesus, we find a similar manifestation of the Spirit. As the Spirit equipped Jesus for His ministry, so it is with the people of Jesus.

The meaning of Pentecost

The remarkable and supernatural events that occurred on the day of Pentecost caused the wondering crowds to ask, 'What does this mean?' It would be difficult to answer the question more succinctly than to say that it was the fulfilment of a promise, the experience of a power and the indwelling of a Person.

The fulfilment of a promise

In his flaming and convicting sermon, Peter claimed that this promise of the Old Testament prophet Joel had now seen its fulfilment.

> In the last days, God says, I will pour out my Spirit on all people. Your sons and daughters will prophesy, your young men will see visions, your old men will dream dreams. Even on my servants, both men and women, I will pour out my Spirit in those days, and they will prophesy (Acts 2:17-18).

This promise of an outpouring of the Spirit was supported by a further promise from the Lord Himself: 'In a few days you will be baptised with the Holy Spirit' (Acts

1:5). With this prospect of an imminent fulfilment of Joel's prophecy, the disciples obediently waited with palpitating hearts in the Upper Room.

Further, it was the promise of the Father to the Son. 'I am going to send you what my Father has promised,' Jesus told His disciples (Lk 24:49).

So on that memorable day the Father fulfilled His promise to His Son, and the Son fulfilled His promise to His disciples.

The experience of a power

Although the apostles had enjoyed the privilege of three years of concentrated individual instruction from the Peerless Teacher, their lives were characterized more by weakness and failure than by power and success. But Pentecost changed all that. Jesus assured them that this defect would soon be remedied. 'You will receive power when the Holy Spirit comes on you; and you will be my witnesses' (Acts 1:8).

Innate in human nature is the craving for power, but power in itself is not always a blessing. Evil men can possess and exercise power. The devil has great power, but it is not accompanied by purity and humility—that is why he is what he is. The power the disciples received came direct from the throne of God by the hand of the glorified Lord. It was supernatural and transforming, and qualified them to be humble yet courageous witnesses to Him. Now we read that Christ's disciples were 'full of power'.

The indwelling of a Person

This was the real heart of the Pentecostal event. Jesus had promised, 'The Spirit . . . lives with you and will be in you' (Jn 14:17). This meant nothing less than the personal and permanent indwelling of the other Comforter of whom Jesus had spoken. Not a power, not an influence, not an emanation, but a divine Person who would bring with Him

His own powers and attributes. *This, and not the spectacular miracles, was the true focus of Pentecost.*

The supernatural signs

'Men try to psychologize, demythologize, anything to get rid of the supernatural—the idea of a personal God operating in history,' wrote James S. Stewart. God is denied the liberty to act as He will in His own creation. But the supernatural in religion cannot be excluded.

In His wisdom, God accompanied the gift of the Holy Spirit with audible and visible signs that marked it as a supernatural visitation. There was no literal wind or fire. The sound that came from heaven was only *like* the rush of a mighty wind. The tongues that appeared were tongues *as of fire*. Why were these the symbols chosen to represent the coming of the Holy Spirit? The former Archbishop of Canterbury, Lord Coggan, graphically suggests the reason:

'A noise like that of a strong driving wind . . . tongues like flames of fire dispersed among them, and resting on each one' (Acts 2:2-3, NEB). How very alarming! Nature's two most devastating agents. Have you ever seen a beautiful structure razed by fire? Have you ever been in the path of a hurricane? If you have, you will not easily sentimentalize about these elements. And maybe you will think again before you sing

> And His the gentle voice we hear,
>   Soft as the breath of even,
> That checks each thought and calms each fear
>   And speaks of heaven.

Gentle? It was a gale! Soft? It blew to pieces their old and most cherished patterns of life. They found themselves blown into a perfect vortex of problems. And the fire, while it warmed the chill, had an awesome way of burning the dross . . . Fire ravages and rages. If you are playing for safety, do not play with fire.[3]

In Taiwan, I once experienced a typhoon when the wind finally reached a velocity of 200 miles per hour. It was an awesome experience and the devastation was widespread. Wind is unpredictable, irresistible, inscrutable and sovereign in its operation. So it is with the operations of the Holy Spirit.

Also witnessed in Singapore was a raging fire that in a few minutes rendered a thousand people homeless, leaving only ashes and twisted iron. Fire is awful in its devouring fury. It consumes all that is combustible and leaves only that which is indestructible. So it is with the Spirit of burning who consumes the dross and chaff of character and devours carnality and sin. In addition, the same fiery baptism on the day of Pentecost fused the disciples into one body to become a mighty evangelizing agency.

The terrible conditions in the world today, and the carnality often tolerated within the Church, would indicate that only a mighty power like this is adequate to arrest the downward drift.

Speaking in other tongues

What was the purpose behind the disciples' speaking in tongues not previously learned? The objective was not primarily *ecstatic,* although that element was undoubtedly present. Rather it was *evangelistic.* The reason is given in Acts 2:5,9-11.

As the time for the descent of the Holy Spirit, God chose the occasion when Jews from sixteen districts, from the Nile Valley and Rome to the remote East, would assemble in Jerusalem for the Feast of Pentecost. Had the gift of tongues not been given, only those who knew the colloquial language in use in Palestine would have heard the Good News.

The purpose of the tongue-speaking was evangelistic, not in the sense that they necessarily preached the gospel in those tongues. 'We hear them declaring *the mighty works of God,'* with the result that the people were bewildered (v.6), amazed and marvelling (v.7), perplexed (v.12) and mocking (v.13). The miracle evidenced the presence of supernatural, divine power and paved the way for Peter's proclamation of the Gospel message.

Hearts and minds were now open to hear the explanation and application of the recent happenings that had stirred Jerusalem to its core. Here was an irresistible combination—*Man's voice—God's Word—the Spirit's power.* This is still the prescription for revival.

Peter's fire-touched tongue poured out burning logic and fervent appeal from the Scriptures, and the Holy Spirit did the rest. Three thousand people were cut to the heart, repented and believed. The great objective of the Holy Spirit on this occasion was to make the Gospel intelligible to a racially mixed audience, and the miracle was that each one heard in his own language.

In passing it should be noted that, while there is comparison between the tongue-speaking at Pentecost and that at Corinth, there is also contrast.

At Pentecost, all spoke in tongues (Acts 2:4).

This was not true at Corinth (1 Cor 12:30).

At Pentecost, the tongues were understood by all (Acts 2:6).

At Corinth they were understood by none (1 Cor 14:2).

At Pentecost they spoke to men (Acts 2:6).

At Corinth they spoke to God (1 Cor. 14:2, 9).

At Pentecost no interpreter was necessary (Acts 2:6).

At Corinth tongue-speaking was forbidden if no interpreter was present (1 Cor 14:23, 28).

At Pentecost tongues were a sign to believers (Acts 11:15).

At Corinth they were a sign to unbelievers (1 Cor 14:22).

At Pentecost strangers were filled with awe (Acts 2:7-8).
   At Corinth strangers would say they were mad (1 Cor 14:23).
At Pentecost there was harmony (Acts 2:1).
   At Corinth there was confusion (1 Cor 14:33).

Since there is such a divergence between these two manifestations of the gift of tongues, it would be a very questionable procedure to build a system of doctrine solely on the identity of the two occurrences.

It must strongly be emphasized that these supernatural happenings were not the essence of the Pentecostal experience, but only the accompaniments. They were not repeated. The focal point of the day of Pentecost was *the communication of the Holy Spirit to the waiting disciples.* Henceforth His ministry would not as hitherto be local and occasional, but permanent. His ministry would no longer be to a specially selected few, but to as many as the Lord called.

The gift of the Holy Spirit, this heavenly outpouring, can never be and need never be repeated. We might just as well look for a second Calvary. *But all that Pentecost initiated and stands for can be and should be perpetuated in an obedient church.*

The achievements of Pentecost

Pentecost was a notable watershed in the religious history of the world. The river of living water, already flowing, became an irresistible torrent. The greatest transformation was effected in the lives of the Lord's disciples themselves. They were already regenerate, but were in so many ways unlike their Master.

What new thing did Pentecost achieve? What difference did it make in the lives of Christ's disciples and of those who believed through their word? What did the Spirit bring into their lives?

1. First and foremost, *the ascended Christ suddenly became vividly real to them.* They displayed an overwhelming sense of His personal presence with them. The thought of His departure had earlier filled them with dismay, but now they were filled with joy at the reality of His invisible presence, and preached as though He were at their elbow.

2. A few days previously they had been quaking with fear behind closed doors. Their enemies were so many and so influential, and their resources so few. Now they were *able to engage in fearless witness,* although their lives were in jeopardy. 'They were all filled with the Holy Spirit and spoke the word of God boldly' (Acts 4:31).

3. They had all displayed selfish ambition and hunger for power and position. James and John had lobbied for the highest posts in the kingdom and the others had been indignant because they had been forestalled! But now *they were all willing to submerge themselves* and engage in a team ministry.

4. They had been strangely obtuse and 'slow of heart to believe all that the prophets have spoken' (Lk 24:25). They had failed to discern in the plain prophecies of the Old Testament the concept of a suffering Messiah. But now *they received a new insight into Scripture.* In joyous amazement Peter saw new meanings in old prophecies: 'This is what was spoken by the prophet Joel!' he exclaimed. In his extempore sermon, under the illumination of the Holy Spirit, he linked Scriptures that he had never before associated with one another.

5. In spite of the Lord's assurance that He had given them authority to overcome 'all the power of the enemy' (Lk 10:19), they had found themselves strangely powerless in the presence of satanic power. 'Why could not we cast him out?' they had asked Jesus. But *now they were 'full of power'.* The Lord had told them to wait in Jerusalem until they were endued with power from on high. They obeyed,

and with the descent and filling of the Spirit the promised power had come.

6. In their previous ministry, there appeared to be little of the authority that attended the words of their Master. Little is recorded to indicate that their ministry had caused much of a stir. But now, with Spirit-given words, *they were able to present the truth concerning Christ with tremendous power and incisiveness*. It was authoritative preaching that produced deep concern. 'They were cut to the heart' (Acts 2:37). Their hearers were filled with awe and fear, for they sensed the awe-full presence of the Holy God in their midst.

The purpose of Pentecost

The great importance of the event can be gauged by the multiform purpose Christ had in view. It was a crucial moment in the progress of His plan.

A new era was to be ushered in—the dispensation of the Holy Spirit as the Vicegerent of Christ on earth.

It authenticated the apostles as His accredited messengers.

It indicated that their converts were true members of Christ's universal Church.

Henceforth the Spirit's ministry was to convict and convince men of the truth about Jesus.

The outpouring of the Spirit brought into being the New Testament Church of which Christ is the Head, and through which He could continue to express Himself and achieve His world purpose.

It marked the inauguration of the Holy Spirit as the Administrator of the newly-formed Church, and the Chief Strategist of the missionary enterprise.

It constituted the Church the temple of the Holy Spirit, in which He took up permanent residence.

It secured for believers the continual and universal presence of Christ through the Spirit. The temporary gave way to the permanent, and the local to the universal. They exchanged His physical presence for His omnipresence.

It gave in miniature a foreview of the universal dissemination of the Gospel through the Spirit.

It made possible the fulfilment of Christ's great commission through the Spirit's empowering and the Church's obedience.

It equipped the Church for age-long conflict.

The appropriation of the power of Pentecost

It is one thing to know of the power released at Pentecost. It is quite another thing to experience it. Our Lord's intention was that the essentials of the pentecostal event might be perpetuated. But how? He told us the secret.

> If you then, though you are evil, know how to give good gifts to your children, how much more will your Father in heaven give the Holy Spirit to those who ask him (Lk 11:13).

Luke's Gospel was written long after Pentecost, but did our Lord make known this wonderful promise to the Church only when it was no longer relevant because the Holy Spirit had already been given? I think not.

It has been pointed out that the expression 'the Holy Spirit'—with the definite article—occurs eighty-eight times in the English New Testament. In the Greek New Testament, however only on fifty-four occasions does it have the definite article—'*the* Holy Spirit.' On thirty-four occasions the definite article is absent—'Holy Spirit'. The difference is not accidental. Where the definite article is present, the reference is to the Holy Spirit *as a Person*. Where the article is absent it refers to *the operations and manifestations of the Spirit*. In Luke 11:13 there is no definite article.

What is the meaning for us? Since the Holy Spirit was

given on the day of Pentecost, there is no need for us to ask for the Holy Spirit *as a Person*. He is already dwelling in our hearts. 'If anyone does not have the Spirit of Christ, he does not belong to Christ' (Rom 8:9). But the Lord's promise is still open to us. We are free to ask our bountiful heavenly Father *for any operation of the Spirit which we need to enable us to glorify God and fulfil the ministry He has entrusted to us*. It is in this very connection that our Lord said, 'Ask and it will be given to you; seek and you will find' (Lk 11:9).

Which special operation of the Spirit do we need? Is it love? He is the Spirit of love. Is it joy? He will give 'joy in the Holy Spirit'. Is it holiness we need? He is the Spirit of holiness. Do we feel weak? He is the Spirit of power. Are our lives lacking in discipline? The fruit of the Spirit is discipline. The possibilities are endless.

Here is an open cheque which can be cashed at the bank of heaven in any hour of need. *How much more* will your Father in heaven give the needed operation of the Spirit to those who ask Him. Ask and you will receive.

The next step in the development of the missionary idea was the church in Antioch. God had to have a new centre from which to send out the great missionary movement. Jerusalem was too conservative and too exclusive, and so in Antioch a new centre was started and a new mother church was formed, consisting of spirits like Barnabas, the noble merchant prince; Saul, the educated teacher; Manaen, the courtly gentleman; Simeon, the consecrated negro; Luke, the largehearted cosmopolitan, and such men as these, with a large mass of common people that had been brought into the church not even by apostolic preaching, but by the simple testimony of men and women like themselves.[1]

A.B. Simpson

12

The Purpose of Christ's Church

For a whole year [they] met with the church and . . . the disciples were first called Christians at Antioch (Acts 11:26).

Pentecost can be said to be the birthday of the Christian church in the city of Jerusalem. To it was committed the responsibility for carrying out the commission Jesus had given during those forty days. In the gift of the Holy Spirit, He provided the necessary dynamic to enable its fulfilment.

For some time the church enjoyed continuous revival, but it failed to realize its full potential in spreading the Good News to Judea, Samaria and the remote parts of the earth. It was left to another church, not founded by apostles and knowing none of the supernatural events that accompanied the constitution of the Jerusalem church, to fully carry out the Lord's commission. It would be of value to examine some of the elements that contributed to the effective witness of that church.

The New Testament is, in essence, the record of a remarkable missionary movement. Almost all the writers were themselves missionaries, living under a totalitarian regime with marked similarities to those of our own day.

The last book of the New Testament was written in a concentration camp. The Christians of those days were subject to the stresses and strains that exist in many totalitarian regimes in our world at present. The story of the early Church has therefore a great deal of contemporary relevance.

The book of Acts is the first missionary magazine of the Church, and embodies both the history and the philosophy of mission. It is full of typical happenings that have been repeated worldwide down the centuries. It covers a period of thirty years—as though at the beginning of the Christian era God would demonstrate what can be achieved by a body of fallible but dedicated men and women in a single generation.

One church especially came near to the divine ideal, and therefore has a pertinent message for today as well as for yesterday.

Two influential churches

The two churches that exercised the most powerful influence in the first century A.D., were those at Jerusalem and Antioch. The outpouring of the Holy Spirit on the one hundred and twenty on the day of Pentecost, marked the birth of the Jerusalem Church. In the early flush of this transforming experience, continuous revival was experienced. 'The Lord added to their number daily those who were being saved' (Acts 2:47).

The spectacular events accompanying the pentecostal effusion—a sound like a rushing tornado, tongues as of fire, speaking in other tongues—symbolized the irresistible and glowing witness of a Spirit-filled church. It seemed as though the movement would sweep all before it. But the early promise was never fully realized.

The church at Jerusalem

Here they never seemed to grasp the wide sweep and genius of Christ's missionary programme. A narrow racial spirit and a rigid conservatism shackled their outreach. Judea, Samaria and the remote parts of the earth found no place in their myopic vision. Not until persecution forced them to scatter did they move out far from Jerusalem. Even then they failed to pay heed to the command of their ascending Lord: 'You will be my witnesses in Jerusalem, and in all Judea and Samaria, and to the ends of the earth' (Acts 1:8).

It was not the Lord's concept that only when Jerusalem was completely evangelized should they reach out to Judea, and later perhaps to Samaria and finally to the remote parts of the earth. As far as possible, the operation was to be synchronous, but this concept apparently never got through to them.

Tragically, the wave of blessing was confined largely to Jerusalem and to the Jews. But the Lord of the harvest would not allow His missionary purpose to be frustrated. If the privileged trustees of the Good News in Jerusalem would not respond to the impulsion of love, then He must employ the expulsion of persecution to secure His purpose of grace for the Gentiles. Here is the record:

> On that day a great persecution broke out against the church at Jerusalem, and all except the apostles were scattered throughout Judea and Samaria . . . Those who had been scattered preached the word wherever they went (Acts 8:1,4).

But even when they did at last preach the word in Judea and Samaria as Jesus had commanded, they were selective in their audiences. Their exclusive spirit was manifest, for the record says that they 'travelled as far as . . . Antioch, *telling the message only to Jews*' (Acts 11:19, italics mine).

Their Master had said to them, 'I have other sheep that are not of this sheep pen. I must bring them also' (Jn 10:16).

But they said, 'To Jews only.' It took deep suffering and a long period of time to break them of their deep-seated racial prejudice.

Because of their failure, and God's determination to achieve blessing for the whole world of men, another church was brought into being that took Jerusalem's crown.

The church at Antioch

This was destined to set the world aflame with its missionary zeal. Antioch was the third city of the Roman Empire, and was regarded as the Queen city of the East. It eventually became the metropolis of Gentile Christendom. Its founders were unnamed refugee laymen from Cyprus and Cyrene. Of these open-hearted men it is recorded that they 'went to Antioch and *began to speak to Greeks also,* telling them the good news about the Lord Jesus' (Acts 11:20, italics mine). These were men who shared their Lord's vision and spirit, and who took the first steps in supra-racial mission.

The founding of this church was not accompanied by the miraculous events experienced at Jerusalem. The founders were willing to overleap cultural and racial barriers in order to fulfil the Lord's commission, and their obedience released the divine blessing, for 'the Lord's hand was with them, and a great number of people believed and turned to the Lord' (Acts 11:21).

When news of the revival movement reached the church at Jerusalem, they sent Barnabas to Antioch. No more felicitous choice could have been made, for he was 'a son of encouragement', an ideal representative to guide the growing movement. So rapidly did it develop that he was overwhelmed, and additional experienced help to instruct the growing band of converts became urgently necessary.

Whom should he invite for this strategic role? The Holy Spirit guided his mind to make a daring choice. 'He went to

Tarsus to look for Saul'—the former bitter persecutor of the Church. What a magnificent, if risky, choice of a colleague it proved to be! 'So for a whole year Barnabas and Saul met with the church and taught great numbers of people' (Acts 11:26). In the beginnings of the church, exact statistics were given, but by now the Christian movement was getting beyond statistics.

An ideal church

Admitting that this title may be too generous, what distinctive features would justify so high a designation? The church at Antioch came near the ideal in these respects:

It was supra-racial and multi-national

We are probably more sensitive to racial issues today than at any time since the first century. Contemporary world ferment has brought to the light the unjustified arrogance on the one hand, and the justified resentment on the other, of various sectors of the human race, but few solutions are being found to the worldwide problem. Even the Church has not emerged blameless. The Antioch church, however, was gloriously free of racial prejudice and discord. They rejoiced in the fact that God had made from one man 'every nation of men, that they should inhabit the whole earth' (Acts 17:26).

The *cosmopolitan outlook* of the church was reflected in its leadership. Barnabas haled from Cyprus. Simeon and Lucius were black men from Africa. Manaen was of Hebrew or Edomite stock. Saul was a of Tarsus in Cilicia. With such widely-based leadership, Jewish exclusivism was not able to rear its ugly head. Differences of social status were not allowed to mar their unity.

It enjoyed a team ministry

'In the church at Antioch there were prophets and teachers'

(Acts 13:1). These were spiritually gifted men who were able to give definite, systematic and inspirational Bible teaching as well as warm exhortation. Room was made for the exercise of the spiritual gifts of others.

Luke shares with us the manner in which the mind of the Lord of the harvest was communicated. "While they were worshipping the Lord and fasting, the Holy Spirit said, 'Set apart for me Barnabas and Saul for the work to which I have called them'" (Acts 13:2). Here were church leaders who had their priorities right. Their ministry to the people flowed from their worship and ministry to the Lord. The one without the other proves barren and sterile.

The leaders were men who were prepared for discipline and self-denial in the discharge of their spiritual responsibilities. It was while they were fasting that the voice of the Spirit was heard. F.F. Bruce points out that there are indications that New Testament Christians were specially sensitive to the Spirit's communications while fasting.[2]

Scripture is silent as to the exact method by which He made His will known to the group, but it may well have been through one of the prophets to whom the Spirit communicated His will.

It exercised an outward-reaching witness

Some time ago I received a letter from a prominent church leader in Japan who was bemoaning the prevailing attitude in the churches of his country at that time. 'For too long we Japanese have been inward-looking, occupied with ourselves,' he wrote, 'instead of reaching out into the whole world. We need to lift up our eyes and see the white harvest fields.'

This attitude is not peculiar to Japan. J.B. Phillips writes,

> It almost looks as though Christians exist in a closed circle of fellowship with all the members facing inwards, while behind their backs there are millions who long, albeit unconsciously for the gospel, and for the point and purpose in life that only

the gospel can bring.[3]

The church at Antioch avoided this peril by pursuing from the beginning an aggressive evangelistic outreach. So effective was this thrust, that we are told: 'The disciples were first called Christians at Antioch' (Acts 11:26). It was customary in those days for slaves to be called after their master's name, so the nickname 'Christ's ones' stuck to the slaves of Christ. So great was the ingathering of souls, that Chrysostom affirmed that the Christians of Antioch numbered 100,000. Still later, it was estimated that one person in two was a Christian in that city. The record indicates a remarkable movement—'a great number', 'great numbers,' 'the multitude', etc. These men took seriously the Lord's commission to take the Gospel to every creature, and the Spirit poured His blessing on their endeavours.

It practised liberal giving to God

When the prophet Agabus announced to the church that a famine was imminent,

> the disciples, each according to his ability, decided to provide help for the brothers living in Judea. This they did, sending their gifts to the elders by Barnabas and Saul (Acts 11:29-30).

This was the first recorded gift from one church to its counterpart in another land.

From this incident we can learn that the Antioch church did not suffer from the hang-ups prevalent in our day with regard to a supposed conflict between evangelism and social concern. They discharged both responsibilities.

Their generosity was more than an impulsive emotional response to a fervid appeal. It was tested over a period, but they fulfilled their promise. It is easy to feel a transient stirring of the emotions but later to stifle the generous impulse because the will has not been involved.

It viewed prayer as fundamental to the life of the church

Their prayers were not just a pious addendum to their activities, as is so often the case in many churches today. Their service grew out of their praying and therefore gained the blessing of God.

We are not told explicitly what was the burden of the prayers of the church leaders to Acts 13:2, but it is implicit in the answer that came from God. Were they not seeking God's face as to how they were to fulfil His charge to them to 'make disciples of all nations', to carry the Gospel to 'every creature'? He answered their prayers specifically by commanding that they set apart two of their number to spearhead a missionary world movement.

It has been well said that every great movement of the Spirit can be traced back to a kneeling figure. A study of this account shows that the missionaries were discovered, set apart, sent out, supported and welcomed home to the accompaniment of prayer.

It was careful to follow the strategy of the Holy Spirit

It is of more than passing interest in these days of dominating human leadership that in this movement of the Spirit, no dominant leader is obvious. The Holy Spirit was accorded the place of honour, and He was thus able to work mightily because He was unhindered by the carnal ambitions of jealous and unspiritual leaders. He still speaks when we are quiet enough to listen to 'what the Spirit says to the churches'.

In the selection and sending out of the missionaries, the initiative lay not with the church, but with the Holy Spirit. 'The Holy Spirit said, 'Set apart for me Barnabas and Saul' . . . The two of them, sent on their way by the Holy Spirit, went down to Seleucia' (Acts 13:2,4).

Is there not an important lesson for church leaders in this emphasis? Do we really believe and act as if the Holy Spirit still makes His will known to His servants as they earnestly seek His will? Is it that He does not speak today, or is it that church leaders are not sensitive to His voice?

It seems clear that the Spirit had already made His will known individually to Barnabas and Saul before He communicated it to the church. 'Set apart for me Barnabas and Saul *for the work to which I have called them.*' But the two men took no independent action to move forward. They waited until they had the fellowship and co-operation of the church. They did not become rugged individualists, acting without consultation with the church, 'answerable only to God'. The mission fields of the world today are plagued with individuals bent on 'doing their own thing' and creating acute problems both for the national church and fellow missionaries.

The part played by the church is also of interest. The Spirit called on its leaders to verify and concur in the call He had already given to the two men, and then to release them for service. 'They placed their hands on them and sent them off' (Acts 13:3).

It reaped a glorious reward

So too will every church that gives to its missionary programme the priority accorded to it in the New Testament.

Antioch unselfishly spared its most gifted leaders to open up the world to the Gospel, and it became the missionary centre of the world. It was from here the first missionary journey was undertaken. It is not difficult to imagine the jubilation when their own missionaries returned and 'gathered the church together and reported all that God had done through them and how he had opened the door of faith to the Gentiles' (Acts 14:27). True, the church had made a great sacrifice in letting Barnabas and Saul go, but what rich dividends they received!

The secret of success

The question naturally arises as to why the church at
Antioch was so much more successful than the church at
Jerusalem. Was it not that it had grasped and obediently
embraced the spirit of the great commission, and was therefore more in sympathy with the Lord's concern for a whole
world?

Was it not because it was more prayerful in its programme and more Spirit-led in its planning? Was it not
because it was more outward-going in its sympathies and
service? It was because this church gave the missionary
enterprise a paramount place in its heart, that it became
probably the most successful church in history concerning
effective witness in its home city. And herein lies an important lesson for churches in our own day. Evidence
abounds that a wise preoccupation with the work of mis-
sions does not detract from the effectiveness of local work,
but enriches the whole life of the church.

Was there anything so unique and distinctive in this
exemplary church that could not, in measure, be repro-
duced in contemporary churches which are obedient to the
Word of God, and attentive to the voice of the Spirit?

The hope of Christ's return is not just a happy ending to a heart-rending story. Nor is it mere curiosity about the future inventing its own solutions. Without this forward dimension of Christian faith, our assessment of Jesus would be incomplete. Without some form of Advent hope, His Lordship over history remains only an abstract idea.

'Without the Advent expectation, the long story of Christ's suffering and death would lack its ultimate moral vindication—not in reprisal or revenge, but in fulfilment. Without an Advent goal, the course of history seems a dreary vista of endless cycles of sin, suffering and sorrow eternally repeated in a meaningless dance of phantoms'[1]

Reginald E.O. White

13

The Purpose of Christ's Second Advent

I will come back (Jn 14:3).

This same Jesus . . . will come back (Acts 1:11).

During World War Two, General Douglas MacArthur, Commander of the American forces in the Far East, established his headquarters in the Philippines, where he quickly formed very cordial relations with that nation and its leaders. At a time of crisis in the war, he was ordered by his United States government to withdraw his army from the Philippines and deploy his men elsewhere. Fearing the possible tragic consequences such a withdrawal would have for his Filipino friends, he was reluctant to comply. During those dark days, his presence and charismatic leadership had been deeply appreciated by the Filipinos, who had unbounded confidence in him as a man of his word.

He had no alternative, however, but to withdraw. As he was leaving, in a moving farewell speech, he gave the nation this ringing promise and assurance: 'I shall return!' And he did.

These words from a man of undoubted honour and integrity, whom the Filipinos had good reason to trust implicitly, brought to the beleaguered nation desperately-needed hope of ultimate deliverance, a hope that was later fully realized.

On the dark night of our Lord's betrayal, when human perfidy had sunk to its nadir, He opened His heart to His loved friends and shared with them some of the secrets of the future. He commenced His moving farewell address with words so unexpected, so mysterious, that it was only later that their vast implications began to dawn on the bereft disciples.

> I am going there to prepare a place for you. And if I go and prepare a place for you, *I will come back* and take you to be with me that you also may be where I am (Jn 14:2-3, italics mine).

Before many hours had elapsed, the full import of Christ's cryptic words became only too clear. Then they understood what He had meant when He said, 'If I go . . .' But what was the meaning of the mysterious words, 'I will come back'? It was only after the ascension that they had their questions answered by the two angelic visitors who stood beside them as they watched Him ascending into heaven. Their answer was in clear uncomplicated language that a child could understand:

> 'Men of Galilee,' they said, 'why do you stand here looking into the sky? This same Jesus, who has been taken from you into heaven, *will come back in the same way* you have seen him go into heaven (Acts 1:11, italics mine).

The angels' words indicated that the Christ who had risen from the dead and ascended into heaven, would at some future time personally return to the earth, in some manner similar to His departure. As was His going, so would be His coming—visible, literal, corporeal, personal.

> I am waiting for the coming
>   Of the Lord who died for me;

> O His words have thrilled my spirit,
>   'I will come again for thee.'
> I can almost hear His footfall
>   On the threshold of the door,
> And my heart, my heart is longing
>   To be with Him evermore.
>
>   *S.T. Francis*

The scriptures quoted at the head of this chapter do not stand alone in their proclamation of a second coming of Christ to earth. Indeed, they are only two of the 318 instances in which that event is specifically mentioned or referred to in the 210 chapters of the New Testament. This fact alone should impress us with the commanding importance of the theme to Christians in all ages. Its inclusion in all the great creeds of the Christian Church is evidence that the expectation of Christ's return has always formed an integral part of the Church's doctrine.

There is one aspect of the second advent which remains unrevealed, and that is *the time factor*. For that reason, any attempts to predict its exact date are foredoomed to failure. The coming Lord left us in no doubt on this point. *'No-one knows about that day or hour,* not even the angels in heaven, nor the Son, but only the Father' (Mt 24:36, italics mine). In spite of this affirmation, men in their arrogance have repeatedly made their predictions, which have been as repeatedly disproved in the event.

The purpose of the advent

There are compelling reasons that lead us to believe that Jesus will return to earth to receive His Bride and usher in the end of the age.

1. He must return to redeem His own promise. To one who believes the Scriptures to be the inspired Word of God, this is in itself a sufficient reason, since 'He cannot disown Himself' (2 Tim 2:13). Could any promise be more specific than this? 'I will come back and take you to be with me.' Many other statements of the Lord can be interpreted only in terms of His personal return. For example:

> At that time the sign of the Son of Man will appear in the sky.
> . . . They will see the Son of Man coming on the clouds of the sky, with power and great glory (Mt 24:30).

2. *He must return to complete the fulfilment of many Messianic prophecies of the Old Testament.* Luke 4:16-20 is one such prophecy. Returning to Nazareth, following His usual custom, Jesus went to the synagogue. There He read the scripture set for the day—Isaiah chapter 61:

> 'The Spirit of the Lord is on me, because he has anointed me to preach good news to the poor. He has sent me to proclaim freedom for the prisoners and recovery of sight for the blind, to release the oppressed, to proclaim the year of the Lord's favour.'
>   Then he rolled up the scroll, gave it back to the attendant and sat down. The eyes of everyone in the synagogue were fastened on him, and he said to them, 'Today this scripture is fulfilled in your hearing' (Lk 4:18-21.

Why did Jesus stop reading in the middle of verse 21, and sit down without completing the passage? The reason must surely be that, while the first part of the verse had been fulfilled in His first advent, the terrible second part—'and the day of vengeance of our God'—awaited His return at the end of the age for its fulfilment.

3. *He must return to vindicate the prediction of the heavenly messengers at His ascension.* It will be remembered that as Jesus ascended into heaven before the gaze of His astonished disciples, two men in white clothing, in the presence of many witnesses, confidently assured them that His departure was not permanent, that He would return. This prediction must be vindicated.

4. *He must return to complete His work of redemption.* His atoning sacrifice on Calvary for ever redeemed all who

believe from the penalty and power of sin. But there is one aspect of redemption which yet remains to be completed. To Paul, redemption was incomplete apart from the redemption of the body. He wrote, 'We . . . groan inwardly as we wait eagerly for our adoption as sons, the redemption of our bodies' (Rom 8:23).

At present, we are at home in the body, but are absent from the Lord (2 Cor 5:6-8). When Christ returns, body and spirit will be reunited, and our redemption completed (1 Thess 4:16-17).

5. *He must return to confirm the truthfulness and trustworthiness of the Scriptures.* Every New Testament writer without exception bears his witness to the return of Christ to earth. With the exception of the small books, Philemon and 2nd and 3rd John, every book makes reference to it. Paul in his writings speaks of it twenty-seven times, sometimes at considerable length. If Christ did not return, the trustworthiness of the New Testament writings and writers would be irreparably shaken.

6. *He must return to execute judgement on those who have rejected His Gospel and spurned His love.* No one who accepts the authority of Christ and the authenticity of His Word, can doubt that there is judgement to come. For the impenitent, Jesus taught in clearest terms that there is the inescapable prospect of standing before the bar of God. Hear the Lord's own words:

> When the Son of Man comes in his glory, and all the angels with him, he will sit on his throne in heavenly glory. All the nations will be gathered before him, and he will separate the people one from another as a shepherd separates the sheep from the goats (Mt 25:31-32).

John records his vision of the judgement day:

> Then I saw a great white throne and him who was seated on it. Earth and sky fled from his presence . . . and I saw the dead, great and small, standing before the throne, and books were

opened. Another book was opened, which is the book of life
. . . The dead were judged according to what they had done as
recorded in the books . . . If anyone's name was not found
written in the book of life, he was thrown into the lake of fire
(Rev 20:11-12, 15).

No more solemn, awe-inspiring scene is to be found in
the Bible than this event. By inspiration, Paul describes it
in these sombre words:

> . . . when the Lord Jesus is revealed from heaven in blazing fire
> with his powerful angels. He will punish those who do not
> know God and do not obey the gospel of our Lord Jesus. They
> will be punished with everlasting destruction . . . *on the day he
> comes* to be glorified in his holy people (2 Thess 1:7-10).

These and other parallel scriptures require His return to
give effect to the predicted judgement.

7. *He must return to provide the answer to the prayer He
taught His disciples.* 'When you pray,' He counselled them
in response to their request for teaching on this subject,
'this is how you should pray: ". . . your kingdom come,
your will be done on earth as it is in heaven"' (Mt 6:9-10).

But can there be a kingdom without a king? If the kingdom concerning which Jesus spoke so constantly both before and after His resurrection is to be established, then He
must return to show that He reigns, and to rule over all the
world.

What His second advent will mean to Him

In our study of this theme, is it not true that most of us think
more of what its implications will be for ourselves, than of
what it will mean for our coming King? A very popular
gospel song of a generation ago epitomized the current
sentiment:

> O that will be glory for me,
> When by His grace

> I shall look on His face
> That will be glory, be glory for me.

Of course that is blessedly true, but in our self-occupation, do we give adequate thought to what it will mean to Him? We tend to think of it in terms of our personal involvement, but are we equally and intelligently thrilled at what 'His inheritance in the saints' will mean to Him? Is His coronation day prominent in our minds, or is it our deliverance from the woes of this present evil age that is our primary interest?

Alice Janvrin expresses the Lord's attitude to His return:

> He is waiting with long patience
> For His crowning day,
> For that Kingdom which shall never
> Pass away.
> Waiting till His royal banner
> Floateth far and wide,
> Till He seeth of His travail,
> 'Satisfied!'

There are striking contrasts between the attendant circumstances of Christ's first and second advent. He came then in poverty and humiliation. This time He will come in limitless power. He came then alone. This time He will be accompanied by His angels and the redeemed. He came then as Man of Sorrows. This time He will take up and wield the sceptre of universal dominion. Whereas men pressed into His brow a crown of thorns before, this time he will come adorned with the many diadems He has won by His mediatorial work. Whereas He was blasphemed, denied and betrayed before, this time every knee will bow and every tongue acknowledge Him King of kings and Lord of lords.

When He returns, it will be to receive His kingdom. On His first coming to His own people to offer Himself as their King, their response was in effect, 'We will not have this man to reign over us.' But at the last, His kingship will be universally acknowledged and confessed.

His return will also result in His eternal union with His Bride, the Church which He purchased with His own blood. For Him, as for us, there will be the ecstatic joy of the marriage supper of the Lamb, and eternal fellowship with Him (Rev 19:9).

What His second advent will mean to us

> If I go and prepare a place for you, I will come back and take you to be with me that you also may be where I am (Jn 14:3).

The prospect of Christ's imminent return should fill the heart of the disciple who is walking in fellowship with his Lord with exultant joy. In addition to the joy of at last seeing the Lord reigning, worshipped and adored, there will be our own joy and rapture at seeing Him face to face.

For us, too, *it will mean a wonderful transformation:* 'We know that when he appears, we shall be like him, for we shall see him as he is' (1 Jn 3:2).

He will transform the body of our humble state into conformity with the body of His glory (Phil 3:21).

Paul further elucidates what will then take place: 'Listen, I tell you a mystery: We will not all sleep, but *we will all be changed*—in a flash, in the twinkling of an eye, at the last trumpet' (1 Cor 15:51-52, italics mine).

It will be a time of glorious reunion with loved ones who have died in Christ, when

> the Lord himself will come down from heaven, with a loud command, with the voice of the archangel and with the trumpet call of God, and the dead in Christ will rise first. After that, we who are still alive and are left will be caught up with them in the clouds to meet the Lord in the air. And so we will be with the Lord for ever (1 Thess 4:16-17).

It will be the occasion of our perfected sanctification. On earth, our sanctification, our progressive growth in likeness to Christ is a continuing process, and we often mourn that our progress is so slow. But when He appears, the process will be consummated. 'We shall be like Him.' What bliss— to be saved to sin no more! To be delivered from even the presence of sin!

It will mean that death is finally and for ever banished and vanquished, its sting extracted. With our Lord we will live in the power of an endless life. To the believer, death is not death, only 'sleep'. When Christ returns, the believers of that generation will be spared even that 'sleep', 'for we will not all sleep, but we will all be changed in a flash', the dead shall be raised imperishable. Then the saying that is written will come true: 'Death has been swallowed up in victory. Where, O death, is your victory? Where, O death, is your sting?' (1 Cor 15:51-54).

> Who is this that comes in glory,
> With the trump of jubilee?
> Lord of battles, God of armies,
> He has gained the victory;
> He who on the cross did suffer,
> He who from the grave arose,
> He has vanquished sin and Satan,
> He by death has spoiled his foes.
> *Christopher Wordsworth*

What His second advent will mean to Satan

For no one will the return of Christ have greater and more far-reaching significance than for Satan, the evil prince of this world. Scripture presents a consistent picture of two rival kingdoms confronting each other on the world scene —the kingdom of Satan and darkness, and the kingdom of God and light. Satan and his minions are allied with evil men in their plan to smash the kingdom of God's dear Son, and effect the ruin of the human race.

At the end of the age, Satan is seen as allied with the beast and the false prophet. These three, united in a common purpose to defeat Christ and secure domination of the whole world, form a sinister trinity of evil. While on earth, Jesus inflicted a stunning defeat on Satan, first in the temptation in the desert, but pre-eminently in the cross. By His death He 'destroyed—rendered impotent—him that had the power of death, that is the devil'.

It was for this very purpose that Christ came to earth the first time. 'The reason the Son of God appeared was to destroy the devil's work' (1 Jn 3:8). At Calvary that victory was achieved, and the sentence of doom passed.

Ever since Calvary, the vaunted power of the adversary is only as great as the Sovereign God, for His own wise purposes, allows. His power is not inherent. It is not invincible, but vulnerable and shattered; not triumphant, but doomed. He and his accomplices are reserved for a final yet future judgement, which is described in Revelation 20:7-10:

> When the thousand years are over, Satan will be released from his prison and will go out to deceive the nations . . . to gather them for battle . . . And the devil, who deceived them, was thrown into the lake of burning sulphur, where the beast and the false prophet had been thrown. They will be tormented day and night for ever and ever.

> Oh the joy to see Thee reigning,
> Thee our own beloved Lord!
> Every tongue Thy name confessing,
> Worship, honour, glory, blessing
> Brought to Thee with one accord:
> Thee our Master and our Friend,
> Vindicated and enthroned,
> Unto earth's remotest end
> Glorified, adored and owned!
> *Frances R. Havergal*

Index of Persons

Amin, Idi	13	Francis, S.T.	168–169
Andrewes, Lancelot	19		
Augustine of Hippo	120	Ghandi, Mohandas	9
		Gilder, Richard W.	42
Barrett, C.K.	55	Green, Michael	37, 142
Boice, James M.	89		
Bonar, Andrew	19	Harrison, E.F.	51
Borden, William	88	Havergal, Frances R.	48–49,
Bottome, F.	60		86, 176
Brainerd, David	19	Herbert, George	26
Bruce, F.F.	65,160	Howden, J. Russell	92
Buddha	10	Hustwhat, Katherine	43
Bunyan, John	43		
		Janvrin, Alice	173
Chrysostom, John	119		
Clarke, Sir Edward	93	Kantzer, Kenneth S.	23, 27
Coggan, F.D.	144	Kelly, Thomas	21
Conder, Josiah	113		
Confucius	10	Lang, G.H.	135
Court, Lewis H.	95	Lange, J.P.	119
Cowper, William	113	Luther, Martin	102
		MacArthur, Douglas	167
Davies, J.G.	119	Maclaren, Alexander	73
Dionysius	11	Maclaren, Ian	102

Muhammad 10
Mantle, J. Gregory 127
Meyer, Frederick B. 56
Myers, F.W.H. 81
Milton, John 26
Morgan, G. Campbell 34, 47, 70
Morison, Frank 99
Moule, H.C.G. 118
Murray, John 33

Niemoller, Martin 32

Packer, James I. 80, 139
Phillips, J.B. 25, 160

Rawson, George 71–72, 75
Ray, Chandu 15
Renan, Ernest 16
Rieu, E.V. 25
Rimmer, Harry 98

Schaff, Philip 44
Scroggie, W. Graham 115
Simpson, Albert B. 103, 153
Slater, R. 101
Smith, David 41
Smith, Wilbur M. 65
Spurgeon, Charles H. 86
Stewart, James S. 144
Studd, Charles T. 84

Tacitus 29
Taylor, Mrs J.H. 86
Tisseraud, Jean 110
Trench, R.C. 68

Vries, Henry de 131

Watts, Isaac 20
Wells, H.G. 16
Wesley, Charles 119, 131, 132
Westcott, B.F. 45
White, R.E.O. 75, 77, 165
Wordsworth, C. 120, 175

Zoroaster 10
Zwemer 9, 97

Scripture Index

Genesis			6:9-10	172
12:2	137		11:6	19
			12:40	96
Numbers			16:16	69
6:24-26	137		16:28	74
			17:2	67, 71
Job			19:28	9
9:33	130		20:18-19	96
			21:12-13	59
Psalms			21:15	58
22	20		24:30	170
68:18	121		24:36	169
			25:31-32	171
Isaiah			26:38	19
53	20		27:51-53	21
			27:63-66	96
Malachi			28:18	107
3:1-3	62–63		28:20	101

Matthew			Mark	
3:16-17	39		1:12-13	39, 40
4:1	40		2:28	10
4:3, 5, 10	41		8:38	74

9:2-3	67, 71
11:6	61
13:1	55

Luke
1:34-35	31, 32
1:35	12, 44
4:1-2	41
4:13	41
4:14	48
4:18-21	170
9:29	67, 71
9:30-31	70, 73
10:19	107, 148
11:9-10	10
11:13	150
13:11	135
22:27	133
22:40	19
23:44-45	20
24:1-3	97
24:16, 31	106
24:39	94
24:47	111
24:49	143
24:50-51	120

John
1:1	29
1:14	25, 71
2:13-16	53
2:17	62
2:19, 21	95
7:37-38	122
8:46	42
10:18	12
13:3-5	18
14:2-3	168
14:3	125, 167

14:6	12
14:9	34
14:10	13
14:12	124
14:17	143
14:18	101, 120
14:19	124
14:30	42
15:18	85
16:7	120
17:15	85
18:6	57
20:6-7	97
20:8	97
20:17	107, 121
20:19-20	110
21:1	110

Acts
1:2	48, 109
1:2-3	110, 144
1:3	105, 112
1:5, 8	139
1:8	110, 125, 143, 157
1:11	167, 168
2:1-4	141
2:4	146
2:5, 9-11	145
2:6	146
2:17-18	142
2:23	41
2:33	122, 129
2:33-35	129
2:37	149
2:47	156
4:31	148
8:1, 4	157
11:19-21	157-158
11:26	155, 159, 161

11:29-30	161	7:1	57
13:1-2	160	13:14	137
13:2-4	162		
13:3	163	*Galatians*	
14:27	163	1:4	85
17:26	159	4:4	29, 31
17:27	112		
		Ephesians	
Romans		1:19-20	100
1:4	100	1:20-22	122
6:6-7	82	4:8	117, 121, 122
6:17-18	83		
8:9	151	*Philippians*	
8:23	171	2:8-9	123
8:27	133	3:10	100
8:34	124		
10:9	87	*1 Thessalonians*	
14:9	79, 83, 87	4:16-17	171, 174
		4:17	75
1 Corinthians		5:10	86
3:16-17	56		
6:19	56	*2 Thessalonians*	
12:11	122	1:7-10	172
12:30	146		
14:2-9	146	*1 Timothy*	
14:22-23	146, 147	3:16	27
14:23,28	146		
14:33	147	*2 Timothy*	
15:3-4	92	1:10	101
15:4	91	2:13	169
15:6	98, 111		
15:44	94	*Titus*	
15:51-52	174	2:14	80
15:51-54	175		
		Hebrews	
2 Corinthians		2:14-15	101
4:14	101	2:17-18	134
5:6-8	171	2:18	43, 45, 46, 133
5:15	83	4:4-16	43

4:15	46, 134
5:1-2	130
5:4-5	130
7:24-25	135
7:25	129, 133
7:26	131
9:28	34

1 Peter
1:3	101
1:18-19	81

2 Peter
1:4	32
1:16	74
1:16-18	68, 70

1 John
2:1	133
2:2	80
2:16	46
3:2	174
3:8	29, 33, 176
4:9	32
4:10	32
4:14	33

Revelation
1:5	33
1:8	14
1:17	14
1:18	14, 91, 112
8:3-4	136
19:9	174
20:7-10	176
20:11-12, 15	171–172

Notes

Chapter 1
1. Samuel M. Zwemer, *The Keswick Convention*, (Pickering & Inglis 1937) p. 249.
2. Ibid. p. 248.

Chapter 2
1. Kenneth S. Kantzer, 'The Miracle of Christmas'. *Christianity Today* (14th December 1984) p. 15.
2. Ibid. p. 15.
3. G. Campbell Morgan, *The Westminster Pulpit*, (Fleming Revell 1954), Vol. 1 p. 309.

Chapter 3
1. Michael Green, *I believe in Satan's Downfall*, (Hodder & Stoughton 1981) p. 203.
2. David Smith, *The Days of His Flesh*, 8th Ed. (Hodder & Stoughton 1910) pp. 36-37.
3. Everitt F. Harrison, *A Short Life of Christ*, (Eerdmans 1968) pp. 81-82.
4. Philip Schaff, *The Person of Christ*, pp. 35-36.
5. Brooke F. Westcott, *The Epistle to the Hebrews*, 2nd Ed. (MacMillan & Co 1892) p. 59.

6. Reginald E.O. White, *The Stranger of Galilee,* (Arthur James 1961) p. 50

Chapter 4

1. E.F. Harrison, *A Short Life of Christ,* p. 173.
2. Leon Morris, *The Gospel of John,* (Eerdmans 1971) p. 288.

Chapter 5.

1. Wilbur M. Smith, *The Supernaturalness of Christ,* (W.A. Wilde & Co. 1940) p. 165.
2. G. Campbell Morgan, *Crises of the Christ,* p. 229.
3. Alexander Maclaren, *Expositions of Holy Scripture, St. Luke 1-12,* (G.H. Doran & Co. n.d.) p. 284.
4. Reginald E.O. White, *The Stranger of Galilee,* (Arthur James 1961) pp. 113-114.

Chapter 6

1. Reginald E.O. White, *The Stranger of Galilee,* p. 142.
2. James I. Packer, *Knowing God,* (Hodder & Stoughton 1973) pp. 210-211.
3. Mrs Howard Taylor, *Borden of Yale,* (China Inland Mission 1952) p. 65.

Chapter 7

1. James M. Boice, *God the Redeemer,* (Inter-Varsity Press 1978) p. 226.
2. J. Russell Howden, *'Peter and The Risen Lord',* Sunday School Times (23rd April 1927) p. 264.
3. W. Graham Scroggie, *A Guide to the Gospels,* 2nd Ed. (Pickering & Inglis 1948) p. 602.
4. John R.W. Stott, *Basic Christianity,* (Inter-Varsity Press 1958) p. 46.
5. Samuel M. Zwemer, *The Glory of the Empty Tomb,* (Fleming Revell 1947) p. 48.
6. Harry Rimmer, *'The Resurrection of Jesus Christ',* Christian Faith & Life (April 1937) p. 118.
7. Frank Morison, *Who Moved the Stone?* (Faber & Faber 1958) p. 104.

8. F.J. Horsefield, *'The Power of the Resurrection'*, *The Life of Faith* (12th April 1933) p. 273.

Chapter 8
1. Albert B. Simpson, *The Christ of the Forty Days*, (Christian Publications n.d.) pp. 11-12.

Chapter 9
1. W. Graham Scroggie, *A Guide to the Gospels*, p. 620.
2. J.G. Davies, *Dictionary of Christian Theology*, (S.C.M. Press) p. 15.
3. Ibid. p. 16.

Chapter 10
1. J. Gregory Mantle, *Better Things*, (Marshall Bros 1896) p. 34.
2. Henry de Vries, *The Lord's Anointed*, (Marshall Bros 1925) p. 173.
4. George H. Lang, *The Epistle to the Hebrews*, (Paternoster Press 1951) p. 121.

Chapter 11
1. James I. Packer, *Keep in Step with the Spirit*, (Inter-Varsity Press 1984) p. 89.
2. Michael Green, *I Believe in the Holy Spirit*, (Hodder & Stoughton 1974) p. 61.
3. F.D. Coggan, *'Wind and Fire'*, *The Reaper* (24th October 1964) p. 377.

Chapter 12
1. A.B. Simpson, *The Acts of the Apostles*, (Christian Publications n.d.) p. 60.
2. F.F. Bruce, *The Book of Acts*, (Marshall Morgan & Scott 1954) p. 261.
3. J.B. Phillips, *New Testament Christianity*, (Hodder & Stoughton 1974) p. 61.

Chapter 13
1. Reginald E.O. White, *The Stranger of Galilee*, p. 203.

In Pursuit of Maturity

by J. Oswald Sanders

The apostle Paul summarized the goal of his ministry by the words 'that we may present every man mature in Christ'. He was committed to seeing maturity in both his own life and in others.

In the clear and straightforward style that thousands have come to expect and enjoy, J. Oswald Sanders maps out the path to Christian maturity. While not forgetting the trials and disciplines involved, he reminds us of the encouragement and equipping available to us from the Holy Spirit. We also see that the road to maturity can only be followed as we recognize and play our part in the body of Christ.

Kingsway Publications

Focus on Christ

by John Stott

The identity of Jesus Christ is 'news' again—on television and radio, in the papers and on the street. Even within the church there is uncertainty and hot debate.

This book reaffirms the centrality of the risen Jesus to the Christian life. As it explores eight different aspects of our relationship with him, we are encouraged to root ourselves firmly in biblical truth and so grow in our understanding and commitment.

JOHN STOTT is Rector Emeritus of All Souls Church, Langham Place, London; and Director of the London Institute for Contemporary Christianity. A speaker of international renown, he has written over twenty books.

k
Kingsway Publications

The Love Affair

Today's need for love that's real

by Michael Harper

This is a book about perfect love—love that seeks the best for others rather than itself. Love that "bears all things" because it gains its strength from the Source of all true love.

Many today see romantic desire as the highest form of love. But when the New Testament speaks of love, it deliberately avoids the word for sexual love, *eros*. The kind of love God has for us, and that we are to have for one another, is called *agape*. Such love is deliberate and selfless, not based on sentimentality or physical attraction.

In a world where love no longer seems constant, where people's lives are broken by an *eros* love that is uncontrolled and often fickle, we see that it is *agape* love that holds for us the only real hope. This book points the way to such love. Here we see true love in action in God's love for mankind, which is then to be worked out in our own lives by the power of the Holy Spirit.

Kingsway Publications